SPECTRUM

Word Study and Phonics

Grade 4

Spectrum

An imprint of Carson-Dellosa Publishing LLC
Greensboro, North Carolina

Spectrum
An imprint of Carson-Dellosa Publishing LLC
P.O. Box 35665
Greensboro, NC 27425 USA

ISBN 978-0-7696-8294-5

05-151118454

Table of Contents Grade 4

Chapter 1 Phonics

Table of Contents, continued

Chapter 2 Word Structure

Table of Contents, continued

NAME _____

Lesson 1.1 Beginning and Ending Consonants

Look at each picture below. On the first line, write the word that names the picture and circle the beginning consonant. On the second line, write a word from the box that has the same beginning consonant.

| hippo | latch | fox | key |

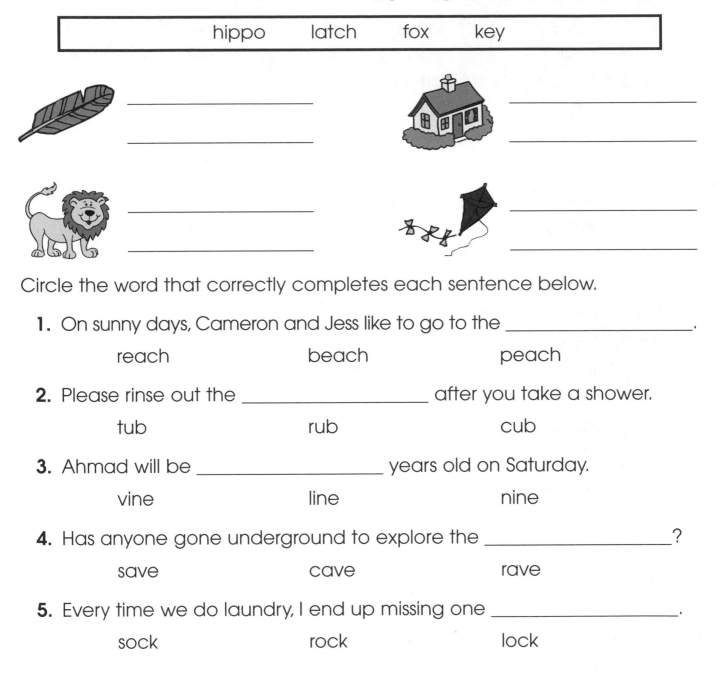

Circle the word that correctly completes each sentence below.

1. On sunny days, Cameron and Jess like to go to the _____.

   reach   beach   peach

2. Please rinse out the _____ after you take a shower.

   tub   rub   cub

3. Ahmad will be _____ years old on Saturday.

   vine   line   nine

4. Has anyone gone underground to explore the _____?

   save   cave   rave

5. Every time we do laundry, I end up missing one _____.

   sock   rock   lock

Lesson 1.1 Beginning and Ending Consonants

Look at each picture below. On the first line, write the word that names the picture and circle the ending consonant. On the second line, write a word from the box that has the same ending consonant.

| grill | mix | hiss | wig | ask | get |

_____
_____

_____
_____

_____
_____

_____
_____

_____
_____

6
_____
_____

Read each word. Change the last letter of the word to make a new word. Write the new word on the line. Your new word should rhyme with the three words below it.

1. stab _____
   car   far   jar

2. trim _____
   rip   sip   skip

3. lisp _____
   fist   wrist   mist

4. fork _____
   sport   short   snort

Lesson 1.2 Hard and Soft **c** and **g**

The letter **c** can make a hard sound, as in car and carrot. When **c** is followed by **e, i,** or **y**, it can make a soft sound, as in center, city, and cycle.

The letter **g** can also make a hard sound, as in goose and give. When **g** is followed by **e, i,** or **y**, it can make a soft sound, as in gentle and ginger.

Read the words in the box. Write each word under the correct heading.

| caring   race   camp   code   cider   cute   ice   rice |

Hard c   **Soft c**

_____   _____

_____   _____

_____   _____

_____   _____

Look at the pictures below. On the first line, write the word from the box that names each picture. On the second line, write hard **g** or soft **g**.

| giraffe   flag   cage   garden |

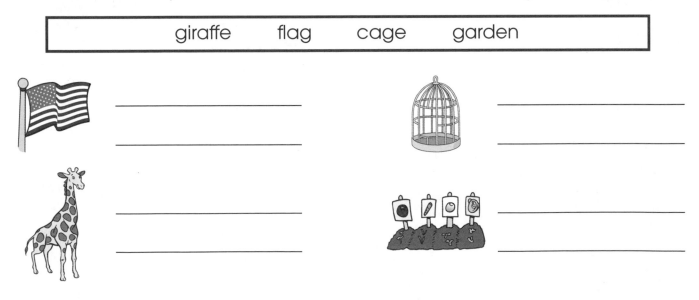

Lesson 1.2 Hard and Soft c and g

Read the pairs of words below. Circle the sound you hear in both words.

1.	guide	gaze	hard **g**	soft **g**
2.	large	badge	hard **g**	soft **g**
3.	code	copper	hard **c**	soft **c**
4.	lace	center	hard **c**	soft **c**
5.	germ	gentle	hard **g**	soft **g**
6.	piece	cellar	hard **c**	soft **c**
7.	wig	tiger	hard **g**	soft **g**
8.	clam	cape	hard **c**	soft **c**

Write the word from the box that matches each clue. Make sure that the word has the correct hard or soft **c** or **g** sound.

Egypt	gorilla	mice	grape	crab	celery	bridge	tiger

1. a large, African ape (hard **g**) _____

2. a sea creature that has strong pincers (hard **c**) _____

3. a country in Africa (soft **g**) _____

4. a purple fruit that grows on a vine; often used to make jelly or juice (hard **g**) _____

5. a piece of metal or wood that allows people to cross over water (soft **g**) _____

6. a type of crunchy, light green vegetable (soft **c**) _____

7. a large wild cat that has orange and black stripes (hard **g**) _____

8. the plural form of mouse (soft **c**) _____

Lesson 1.2 Hard and Soft **c** and **g**

Read each word in bold below. Decide whether it has a hard or soft **c** or **g** sound. Then, underline the word beside it that has the same sound.

1. **certain**	crab	color	fancy
2. **dog**	cage	germ	ago
3. **picnic**	candle	police	once
4. **huge**	grape	bridge	wagon
5. **crazy**	nice	celery	camera
6. **village**	gem	tag	gold

Look at each pair of pictures. Draw a line to match the hard or soft sound to each picture.

1. soft **c**

    hard **c**

2. soft **g**

    hard **g**

3. soft **c**

    hard **c**

4. soft **g**

    hard **g**

Lesson 1.2 Hard and Soft c and g

Read the paragraphs below. Look for words with the hard and soft **c** and **g** sounds. Then, write the words in the correct columns. You do not need to list the same word more than once.

Kids around the world of all ages like to play games. There is a popular game in India that is similar to the American game of tag. The Indian game is called Kabaddi. The players are divided into two teams. If you like, you can flip a coin to see which team will start the game.

Use a large piece of rope to make a line that divides the teams. The teams line up in the center, one on either side of the rope. Team one sends a player over to the other side. The team one player has to try to tag a player from the other team while saying the word Kabaddi over and over again without taking a breath. If the player takes a breath, he or she can be tagged out by a player from team two. If the player makes it to his or her own side without taking a breath, the player is safe. The goal of the game is to be the last player left. If you're fast on your feet and good at running, you'll be great at Kabaddi.

Hard c	Soft c	Hard g	Soft g
_____	_____	_____	_____
_____	_____	_____	_____
_____		_____	
_____		_____	
		_____	
		_____	
		_____	

Lesson 1.3 The Sounds of s

The letter **s** can make different sounds.
- It can make the /s/ sound you hear sink.
- It can make the /z/ sound you hear in music.
- It can make the /sh/ sound you hear in sure.
- It can make the /zh/ sound you hear in treasure.

Read the sentences below. Underline the word or words in parentheses ( ) that best complete each sentence.

1. My family is (always, please) (busy, easy) during the week.

2. We are not (sold, usually) able to eat dinner together.

3. That (is, was) why we make (sugar, sure) to have the Jenkins' Family Game Night once a week.

4. (September, Saturday) and Sunday are the two (does, days) that work (best, last) for everyone.

5. We order a (cheese, grass) pizza, make a (salad, softball), and put some (present, music) on the (stove, stereo).

6. We (slip, stack) our favorite games on the kitchen table and share our (wise, news) from the week.

7. There is no way to (casual, measure) the good (climbs, times) we have during game night.

8. I think (tease, these) are the kinds of (classes, traditions) I will have with my own kids one day.

Lesson 1.3 The Sounds of s

Read each word in bold below. Circle the word beside it that has the same sound of **s**. If you are not sure, try saying the words out loud.

1. **kiss**   singing   shoulder   shock
2. **poison**   sure   snake   yours
3. **casual**   sink   measure   has
4. **sure**   slime   surfer   sugar
5. **tease**   those   usual   sloppy
6. **whistle**   kids   hers   silly

Read the sentences below. On the line, write the **s** sound you hear for each word in bold. Choose from **s** (as in slide), **z** (as in news), **zh** (as in casual), and **sh** (as in sugar).

1. The name **dinosaur** _____ **comes** _____ from a word that means terrible lizard.

2. About 65% of dinosaurs were herbivores, or plant **eaters** _____.

3. Pterodactyls were flying reptiles. **Some** _____ had a wingspan 40 feet long.

4. The triceratops had three **horns** _____ and was twice as big as a rhino.

5. The stegosaurus had sharp **spikes** _____ on its tail.

6. Finding a **fossil** _____ can be like digging up a **small** _____

   treasure _____.

Review Beginning and Ending Consonants, Hard and Soft c and g, and the Sounds of s

Read the sentences below. Fill in each blank with a consonant to complete the word. The words you form should make sense in the sentences.

1. Having a _____ aseball card collection can be a fu_____ hobby for a

   basebal_____ fan.

2. Between 1869 and the 1930s, _____ards were often _____old in a

   pack with _____andy or gu_____.

3. Paper was in shor_____ supply during World _____ar II, so cards were

   har_____ to ge_____ at that _____ime.

4. For a _____ong time, a company calle_____ Topps was the only
   company to produce baseball cards.

5. In the 1980s, a lot more _____eople became interested in

   _____ollecting.

6. _____oday, four companies are allowed to make cards of the Major

   League _____layers.

Say each word in bold to yourself. If it has a hard sound (like club or great), circle hard. If it has a soft sound (like lace or age) circle soft.

1. **uncle**	hard	soft	5. **camera**	hard	soft
2. **slice**	hard	soft	6. **guide**	hard	soft
3. **gold**	hard	soft	7. **engine**	hard	soft
4. **George**	hard	soft	8. **cellar**	hard	soft

Review Beginning and Ending Consonants, Hard and Soft **c** and **g**, and the Sounds of **s**

Look at each picture below. On the first line, write the word that names the picture. Then, write the words from the box with the same hard or soft **c** or **g** sound under the correct headings.

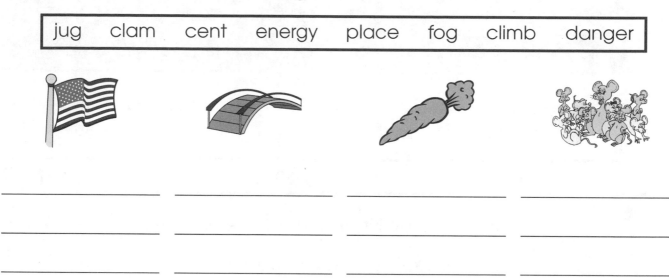

| jug | clam | cent | energy | place | fog | climb | danger |

Read the sentences below. The information in parentheses will tell you which sounds of **s** to look for and how many words to circle in each sentence.

1. The double-decker bus is a bus that has two levels. (/s/ sound, 2)

2. They are a popular way for visitors to see a town. (/z/ sound, 1)

3. The most famous double-decker buses were found in England. (/s/ sound, 3)

4. They were shiny red and seated about 60 to 80 passengers. (/s/ sound, 2) (/z/ sound, 1)

5. In 2005, most of the remaining double-deckers in England were retired. (/s/ sound, 1)

6. Two routes in London continue to use the old two-story buses to preserve a treasured piece of history. (/zh/ sound, 1) (/z/ sound, 3)

Lesson 1.4 Beginning Two-Letter Blends

Some words begin with two consonants. When the sounds of the consonants are blended together, the two letters are called a **blend**.

Each of the words below has an **s** blend (**s** plus another consonant).

scale   **sk**in   **sm**ooth   **sn**uggle   **sp**arkle   **st**ore   **sw**ing

Read each meaning below. Choose a word from the box that matches the meaning. Write the word on the line.

sneeze	stegosaurus	spinach	scale

1. _____ something that measures weight

2. _____ a leafy green vegetable

3. _____ something people do when they have a cold

4. _____ a dinosaur that had bony plates on its back

Underline each word that begins with an **s** blend in the sentences below. Then, circle the blend.

1. Stella and Spencer put on sweaters and wrapped scarves around their necks.

2. They spent every fall evening swinging from the old oak tree.

3. Stella scanned the sky for constellations. Stella and Spencer were keeping score to see who could spot more stars.

4. Spencer liked the way the air smelled like smoke from backyard bonfires.

5. When it was time to go back inside, Stella and Spencer snuggled into their beds. They knew that snow was coming, and fall would soon be over.

Lesson 1.4 Beginning Two-Letter Blends

Some blends are made with **l** plus another consonant. Each of the words below has an **l** blend (a consonant plus **l**).

blink   **cl**ose   **fl**ight   **gl**ass   **pl**ate   **sl**ope

Read each meaning below. Choose a word from the box that matches the meaning. Write the word on the line.

slippers	black	slow	flossing	clothing	glass	plum

1. _____ the opposite of fast

2. _____ a deep purple fruit that tastes both sweet and tart

3. _____ using a small piece of string to clean in between the teeth

4. _____ the things you wear every day

5. _____ the shiny, clear part of a window is made of this material

6. _____ the type of shoes one might wear with pajamas

7. _____ the color that is the opposite of white

Underline the **l** blend in each word below. Then, draw a line to match each word with another word that begins with the same **l** blend.

1. bleach   classic

2. flame   glitter

3. plaid   blouse

4. cliff   plump

5. glance   flatten

Lesson 1.4 Beginning Two-Letter Blends

Some blends are made with **r** plus another consonant. Each of the words below has an **r** blend (a consonant plus **r**).

brain   **cr**adle   **dr**ill   **fr**ee   **gr**ass   **pr**epare

Read the silly sentences below. Circle each **r** blend. Then, write another word with the same **r** blend on the line.

1. Georgia, the graceful grasshopper, likes to nap on a patch of green grass on the ground. _____

2. The prince and princess are prisoners who are given only pretzels and prunes to eat. _____

3. Drew, the dreadful dragon, is a drummer for a band called the Dizzy Dragonflies. _____

4. Every day, Brittany brushes and braids her hair on the bridge by the brook. _____

5. Crabs, crayfish, and other critters creep and crawl across the ocean floor. _____

Solve each problem below. Write the new word on the line.

1. grill - gr + dr = _____

2. drag - dr + br = _____

3. greed - gr + fr = _____

4. fridge - fr + br = _____

Lesson 1.4 Beginning Two-Letter Blends

Two blends that are less common are **tw** and **qu**.

twice   **tw**inkle   **qu**ake   **qu**iz

Look at each picture below. Choose the word or words from the box that name the picture and write them on the line.

| two | quarterback | twirl | question mark | quotes | twig |

Read each sentence below. On the line, write a word from the box that makes sense in the sentence.

| Queen | quilts | twelve | twins | twenty | quails |

1. Queen Tess and Queen Bess were _____, and no one could tell them apart.

2. They were only _____ years old, but they would rule the

   kingdom of Quincy when they turned _____-one.

3. _____ Bess raised _____, which are small, plump birds.

4. Queen Tess liked to sew patchwork _____ with scraps of her favorite fabrics.

Lesson 1.5 Beginning Three-Letter Blends

Some words begin with three consonants. Blend the sounds of the consonants together when you say the words. Each of the words below starts with a three-letter blend.

scream   **spl**ash   **spr**int   **squ**ash

Read the ads below. Fill in each blank with a word from the box that makes sense in the ad.

spread	squirrels	sprain	square dancing	split	screws	squeaky

1. Scoopers uses fresh ice cream and makes the best banana

   _____ in town!

2. Bring your dog into Pet World on Saturday and get a free

   _____ toy.

3. _____ our creamy cream cheese on your bagels for a real treat.

4. Do _____ eat all your birdseed? Buy our special "birds-only" feeder for just $19.99.

5. Come to Jeb's Little Valley Hardware Store. We have hammers, nails,

   _____, toolboxes, and everything else to meet your hardware needs.

6. If you _____ an ankle or break a leg, get your crutches at Grady Medical Supplies.

7. You don't have to live in the country to enjoy _____. Just grab a partner and come on down to Dale's Dance Studio!

Lesson 1.5 Beginning Three-Letter Blends

Each of the words below has a new three-letter blend. Remember to blend the sounds of the consonants together as you say the words.

stripe   **shr**ub   **thr**ill

Read the sets of words below. Circle the word in each set that does not begin with the same three-letter blend as the other words.

1. strict   squeeze   strain
2. thrush   throw   thought
3. spread   shrug   shriek
4. strong   splinter   strum
5. think   threat   thrill
6. shrivel   scribble   shrank

Read each clue below. Underline the word in parentheses that matches the clue. Circle the three-letter blend in the word you choose.

1. a type of seafood (shrimp, shrub)
2. thin string used for sewing (threat, thread)
3. a sweet, red, summer fruit (strawberry, streamer)
4. another word for creek or brook (scrape, stream)
5. to tear into tiny pieces (squawk, shred)
6. another word for road (streak, street)
7. what you use to swallow (throat, three)
8. the opposite of crooked (straight, split)

Lesson 1.6 Ending Blends

Some blends come at the ends of words. Blend the two consonants together when you say the words. Each of the words below has an ending blend.

shi**ft**   fau**lt**   cha**mp**   wi**nk**   be**nt**   a**sk**   du**st**   ki**nd**

On the first line, write the ending blend that completes each picture's name. On the second line, write a word from the box that has the same blend.

crust	salt	lift	trunk

spacecra_____

_____

li_____

_____

be_____

_____

chipmu_____

_____

Solve each problem below. Write the new word on the line.

1. bend - nd + lt = _____

2. draft - ft + nk = _____

3. blank - nk + st = _____

4. task - sk + rt = _____

5. fist - st + nd = _____

Lesson 1.6 Ending Blends

Here are some more words that have ending blends.

help   art   child   fact   kept   bird   stork   wasp

Underline the ending blends in the words below. Then, draw a line to match each word with another word that ends with the same blend.

1. pact   except

2. kept   scalp

3. pitchfork   skirt

4. hurt   exact

5. gulp   bark

Read the letter below. Choose the ending blend in parentheses that best completes each word and write it on the line.

Dear Francisco,

      This postca_____ (rd, lp) is from North Carolina. On the way here, we passed through some towns with funny names: Liza_____ (pt, rd) Lick, Bat Cave, and Frying Pan Landing. We visited the Cape Hatteras lighthouse, a popular landma_____ (rk, lp). We watched wi_____ (ld, lp) dolphins playing in the ocean. I even tried some cri_____ (ld, sp) fried shrimp.

See you soon—Logan

p.s. I bought you a cool T-shi_____ (pt, rt) at a national pa_____ (rk, sp).

Francisco Vargas
940 E. Barker Dr.
Pittsburgh, PA 15218

Review Beginning and Ending Blends

Look at each picture below. Add a beginning blend from the box to complete each word so that it names the picture.

qu	sc	gl	st	cr	bl

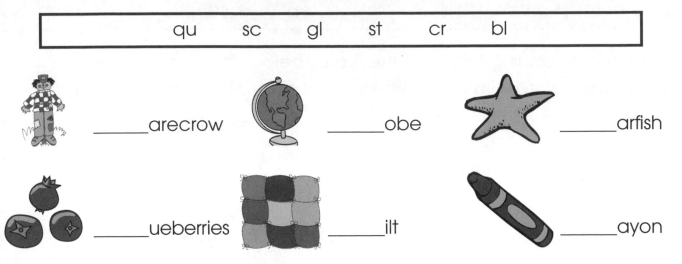

_____arecrow   _____obe   _____arfish

_____ueberries   _____ilt   _____ayon

Read each word in bold below. Underline the word beside it that has the same beginning blend.

1. **sweet**	scan	switch	snug
2. **plaster**	plumber	pinch	sleep
3. **gravity**	free	great	present
4. **twig**	twist	queen	tower
5. **block**	clutch	slice	blonde
6. **snack**	scale	snarl	smog
7. **quake**	twenty	quart	shake
8. **stem**	statue	ski	swarm
9. **treat**	crab	brick	trailer
10. **skate**	sketch	scoot	sharp
11. **pride**	frost	prepare	dragon
12. **clue**	copy	sleepy	cluster

Review Beginning and Ending Blends

Read the sentences below. Fill in each blank with a three-letter blend from the pair in parentheses. The word you form should make sense in the sentence.

1. Mrs. Caldwell thought it was a (spl, squ) _____endid idea for us to paint a mural on one wall of the community center.

2. Aidan painted some trees and (shr, str) _____ubs, and Sophie painted a (scr, squ) _____irrel holding an acorn.

3. Darius tripped on a brush and (str, thr) _____uggled not to lose his balance.

4. Mei (spl, shr) _____ieked as a can of red paint was flung toward the mural.

5. I (thr, squ) _____ew myself in front of the flying paint.

6. The mural was saved, but I'll be (spr, scr) _____ubbing red paint out of my hair for days.

Read the clues below. Fill in the blank with the word from the box that matches each clue. Then, circle the ending blend.

lifeguard	sand	fact	bank	eggplant

1. something that can be proven true; not an opinion _____

2. what a beach is covered with   _____

3. a place people can store their money   _____

4. a person whose job is to keep swimmers safe   _____

5. a large vegetable that is a deep purple color   _____

Lesson 1.7 Beginning Consonant Digraphs

A **digraph** is two letters that make one sound. You do not hear the sound of each letter in a digraph. Together, the letters form a new sound.
- The digraph **sh** makes the sound you hear in short and shave.
- The digraph **ch** usually makes the sound you hear in chair and check.
- The digraph **ch** can also make the /k/ sound you hear in chord and the /sh/ sound you hear in chef.

Circle the beginning digraphs in each sentence below. On the line, write the sound the digraph makes: /sh/ as in shelf and chef; /ch/ as in check; or /k/ as in chord.

1. Charlie and the Chocolate Factory is both a book and a movie.

   _____   _____

2. The movie The Chronicles of Narnia is based on a popular book by

   C. S. Lewis. _____

3. The animated movie Shark Tale stars the voice of Will Smith.

   _____

4. Chris Rock is the voice of Marty the Zebra, the main character in

   Madagascar. _____   _____

5. The book She's Wearing a Dead Bird on Her Head! is based on a true

   story. _____

6. Charlotte's Web is one of the best-loved kids' books of all time.

   _____

Lesson 1.7 Beginning Consonant Digraphs

> • The digraph **th** can make the sound you hear in thin and thread. It can also make the sound you hear in these and though.
> • The digraph **wh** can make the /w/ sound you hear in whine and wheat. It can also make the /h/ sound you hear in who and whole.
> • The digraph **ph** makes the /f/ sound you hear in photo and Philip.

Read each word in bold below. Circle the word beside it that has the same beginning sound.

1. **thirteen**	talking	thought	those
2. **phonics**	flea	police	through
3. **there**	them	thirsty	throw
4. **whenever**	whoever	whisper	whom
5. **whom**	wheel	hospital	whirl

Read the sentences below. One beginning digraph is used several times in each sentence. Find the digraph and circle it each time it is used. Then, think of another word that begins with that digraph and write it on the line.

1. Phoebe the spy used a phony passport to travel from Philadelphia to the Philippines. _____

2. I think that thirty-three people are invited for Thanksgiving dinner. _____

3. When you have finished whisking four eggs, please whip some cream while I set the table. _____

Lesson 1.8 Ending Consonant Digraphs

The digraphs **sh**, **ch**, **th**, and **ph** can come at the ends of words.

tra**sh**   pun**ch**   boo**th**   gra**ph**

Look at the pictures below. On the line, write the ending digraph that completes each picture's name.

digra_____   bru_____   pea_____

mou_____   cou_____   lea_____

Replace the last two letters of each word in bold with the digraph **sh**, **ch**, **th**, or **ph**. Write the new word you form on the line. It should match the definition beside it.

1. **warm**   _____ to clean something

2. **pinto**   _____ to squeeze between two fingers

3. **money**   _____ part of a year; a period of 30 or 31 days

4. **grasp**   _____ a chart that shows a comparison

5. **sound**   _____ the opposite of north

6. **beans**   _____ the sandy area near an ocean or lake

Lesson 1.8 Ending Consonant Digraphs

Complete each sentence below with a word from the box. Circle the digraph in the word.

| phonograph | fourth | paragraph | fish | branch | splash |

1. When writing a paper, each _____ should contain sentences that are about the same topic.

2. The babies _____ water on their parents at the kiddie pool.

3. A huge _____ from the maple tree snapped during the ice storm.

4. The _____ was the most common way of playing music for more than 100 years.

5. For dinner, we ate grilled _____, mashed potatoes, and green beans.

6. Angelina came in _____ at the National Spelling Bee.

Read each set of words below. Underline the words that have the same ending digraph.

1. rich   such   flash   cloth
2. mash   pinch   rush   blush
3. teach   growth   sixth   wish
4. length   autograph   telegraph   search
5. bunch   leash   which   trench
6. path   munch   push   ash
7. finish   tooth   smooth   math

Lesson 1.9 More Ending Consonant Digraphs

Other digraphs, like **ck**, **ng**, and **gh**, can also come at the ends of words.
- The digraph **ck** makes the /k/ sound in truck and snack.
- The digraph **ng** makes the ending sound in string and belong.
- The digraph **gh** can make the /f/ sound in cough and enough.

Look at the pictures below. Write the word from the box that names the picture. Then, circle the word beside it that ends with the same digraph.

laugh	clock	stick	swing

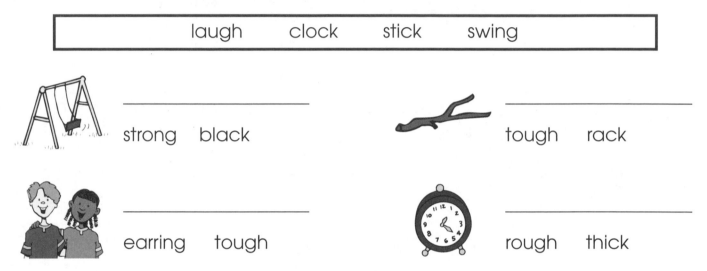

_____   _____
strong   black   tough   rack

_____   _____
earring   tough   rough   thick

Read the paragraph below. Underline the eight words that end with the digraph **ck**, **ng**, or **gh**.

Patricia Polacco has written dozens of picture books. Parts of her life have been rough. For example, her parents got a divorce when she was only three. Patricia had a learning disability and didn't learn to read until she was 14. Still, she loved to draw, and she never forgot to laugh. Looking back on her life, Patricia says that spending time with her grandparents was very important. She learned the art of storytelling by listening to them.

Lesson 1.9 More Ending Consonant Digraphs

Use the clues to match the words in column 1 to their definitions in column 2. Find each word from column 1 in the word search puzzle and circle it.

1. thick   the opposite of old

2. amazing   a small meal

3. enough   plenty

4. snack   a type of jewelry that comes in pairs

5. young   the noise a duck makes

6. cough   ill; not well

7. earring   wonderful; incredible

8. sick   the opposite of thin

9. quack   something you do when you have a cold

q	u	a	c	k	d	g	c	o	s	p
m	k	l	r	w	e	y	o	u	n	g
n	a	a	s	p	t	b	u	c	a	y
o	e	a	r	r	i	n	g	d	c	n
r	n	m	e	i	g	s	h	z	k	p
q	o	a	r	d	u	o	l	s	c	x
n	u	z	w	g	f	o	n	i	v	a
i	g	i	h	y	t	h	i	c	k	b
y	h	n	e	l	l	h	v	k	s	x
v	n	g	p	j	i	d	m	f	t	t

Lesson 1.10 Silent Consonants

In some consonant pairs, one letter is silent.
- The letters **kn** can make the /n/ sound in know. The **k** is silent.
- The letters **wr** can make the /r/ sound in wrap. The **w** is silent.
- The letters **sc** can make the /s/ sound in science. The **c** is silent.
- The letters **mb** can make the /m/ sound in lamb. The **b** is silent.

Read each word in bold. Circle the word beside it that has the same sound as the underlined letters. If you are not sure, say the words out loud.

1. **du<u>mb</u>**   grab   crumb   tub

2. **<u>kn</u>eel**   kiss   karate   never

3. **<u>wr</u>iting**   rules   windy   whisper

4. **<u>sc</u>ience**   scream   scent   crush

5. **to<u>mb</u>**   sob   zoom   crab

Read the sentences below. Choose the word from the box that best completes each sentence. Write it on the line. Then, cross out the silent letter.

climb	knew	limb	wrong

1. As soon as Leah heard the meows, she _____ her cat was stuck in a tree.

2. Daisy thought she could get down alone, but she was _____.

3. "If you help me get the ladder, I can _____ up there and rescue Miss Daisy," said Leah's dad.

4. "Why does she always get stuck on the highest _____?" he asked.

Lesson 1.10 Silent Consonants

Read each meaning below. Choose a word from the box that matches the meaning. Write the word on the line.

wring	scissors	kneel	lamb	wrist
thumb	knit	scientist	writer	knapsack

1. the first finger on the hand _____

2. to sew using two needles and yarn _____

3. a person who is an expert in science _____

4. another word for author _____

5. a young sheep _____

6. a bag carried on the back, like a backpack _____

7. a tool used for cutting; comes in a pair _____

8. the part of the body between the arm and the hand _____

9. to sit on one's knees _____

10. to squeeze or twist water from a piece of cloth _____

Read each word below. Find a rhyming word in the box and write it on the line. Then, cross out the silent letter.

knuckle	limb	scent	knew	wreath	crumb	tomb	knead

1. _____ glum   5. _____ groom

2. _____ stew   6. _____ freed

3. _____ beneath   7. _____ rent

4. _____ chuckle   8. _____ trim

Lesson 1.11 More Silent Consonants

When two or three consonants appear together, one letter is sometimes silent.
- The letters **gn** can make the /n/ sound you hear in sign. The **g** is silent.
- The letters **dg** can make the /j/ sound you hear in judge. The **d** is silent.
- The letters **tch** can make the /ch/ sound you hear in stitch. The **t** is silent.
- The letters **gh** can be silent in the middle or end of a word, as in bright and sleigh.

Read the sentences below. Find and circle the words in each sentence that have one of these letter combinations: **gn**, **dg**, **tch**, or **gh**. Then, circle the word on the second line that has the same combination.

1. The three baby birds would not budge from their perch on the ledge.

   sight   patch   badge

2. Grandma was excited to watch Logan pitch a perfect game.

   ridge   scratch   gnat

3. The puppy sat beneath the gnarled tree and gnawed at a bone.

   design   itch   sigh

4. "Tonight's flight might not be on time," said Manuel.

   pledge   crutch   weigh

5. The patchwork quilt on Julia's bed matches the curtains.

   fetch   assign   midnight

6. The headlights shone straight at the deer that was crossing the road.

   thigh   smudge   badge

Lesson 1.11 More Silent Consonants

Look at the pictures below. Fill in the blanks in the words with the letters **gn**, **dg**, **tch**, or **gh** to form the word that names each picture.

ba____ ____e   flashli____ ____t   wa____ ____ ____

si____ ____   fu____ ____e   slei____ ____

pi____ ____ ____er   midni____ ____t   ju____ ____e

Read each definition and the word beside it. Change the letter or letters in bold to **gn**, **dg**, **tch**, or **gh** to form the word that matches the definition. Write the new word on the line.

1. to promise or vow   ple**as**e _____

2. something to help a person
   with a hurt leg walk   cru**st** _____

3. a disagreement or quarrel   fi**st** _____

4. a small flying insect   **spl**at _____

5. to rub something that itches   scra**pe** _____

Review Digraphs and Silent Consonants

Remember, two letters that stand for one sound are called a **digraph**. Digraphs, like **sh**, **ch**, **th**, and **wh**, can come at the beginning or end of words.

Look at the pictures below. On the line, write the word from the box that names the picture. Then, circle the word below it that has the same digraph.

phone	ring	brush	chef

_____

cough   shout   stick

_____

growth   photo   blush

_____

strong   choir   whine

_____

thick   rough   Chicago

Read the sentences below. Fill in each blank with a digraph from the pair in parentheses. The word you form should make sense in the sentence.

1. Porcupines are rodents, like (sh, ch) _____ipmunks and mice.

2. They are best known for their (th, sh) _____arp quills.

3. To defend themselves, porcupines will swat other animals or bru_____ (ng, sh) against them.

4. The tou_____ (gh, ng), spiky quills sti_____ (ck, ph) in the animal's skin, but they are not poisonous.

5. (Wh, Sh) _____en frightened, porcupines may cli_____ (ng, ck) their

   tee_____ (th, ch) or stamp their feet

Review Digraphs and Silent Consonants

Remember, some consonants can be silent. In the following consonant combinations, the letter in italics can be silent: **kn, wr, sc, mb, gn, dg, tch, gh.**

Look at each picture. The letters beside the picture are scrambled. Unscramble them to form a word that matches the picture. Write the word on the line. Hint: Each word contains a silent letter combination.

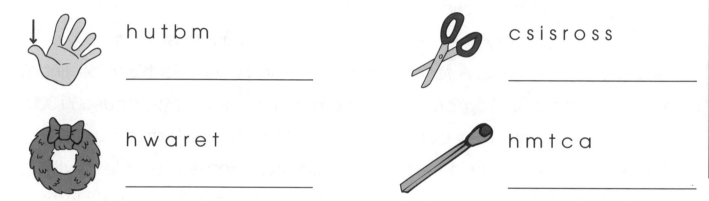

h u t b m

_____

c s i s r o s s

_____

h w a r e t

_____

h m t c a

_____

Read the sentences below. Fill in each blank with a word from the box that makes sense in the sentence. Then, cross out the silent letter in the word.

| judge | knocked | crumb | wrinkled | assign | eyesight |

1. The _____ and jury will hear the case in the courtroom.

2. What homework did Ms. Sachs _____ on Thursday?

3. Jacob _____ on the front door when he arrived at the party.

4. Pugs have curly tails and _____ skin on their faces.

5. Ella reads to her grandpa, who doesn't have good _____.

6. The Devlins' dog catches every _____ that falls to the floor during dinner.

Lesson 1.12 Short Vowels

Read the paragraphs below. Underline the word from the pair in parentheses that has the same short vowel sound as the word in bold beside it.

Are you **fond** (shot, chill) of getting mail? A **pen** (cliff, vest) pal is a person who lives in another city, state, or country. A pen pal **club** (punch, bath) matches students who are about the same age. They **can** (cane, wax) share interests and hobbies. They can learn about what it is like to live somewhere else in the world.

The Student Letter Exchange is the largest pen **pal** (fast, bluff) organization in the world. A teacher wanted to find a way for **his** (hide, finch) students to learn a **lot** (jog, crust) about other cultures. Today, about 500,000 people are members. They come from more **than** (lock, chance) 100 countries. Some pals stay in touch their entire lives. Some are able to **visit** (trip, shred), and others know each other **just** (huge, mug) from their letters. If you **think** (will, rot) you'd like to have a pen pal, visit www.pen-pal.com.

Write a sentence following the instructions in parentheses. You can use the words in the box, or you can use words of your own. Circle the words you use.

stuck	fast	hid	back	jump	when	had	flag	tent	will

1. (2 short **a** words, 1 short **u** word) _____

_____

2. (1 short **i** word, 1 short **e** word, 1 short **a** word) _____

_____

Lesson 1.12 Short Vowels

Read each definition and the word beside it. Change the short vowel sound to form the word that matches the definition. Write the new word on the line.

Ex: to reach out and take   grub   grab

1. fake hair worn on the head   wag _____

2. the part of the body used for walking   log _____

3. ill   sock _____

4. a vehicle used for large or heavy things   trick _____

5. the noise a duck makes   quick _____

6. to come to an end; to halt   step _____

7. a tightly closed hand   fast _____

8. a shelter used for camping   tint _____

Solve each problem below. Write the new word on the line. Then, circle the word beside it that has the same short vowel sound.

1. puck - u + i = _____   brunch   nest   sniff

2. think - i + a = _____   fog   sand   grim

3. shut - u + o = _____   slept   frog   latch

4. flesh - e + a = _____   rung   fox   gasp

5. stuff - u + i = _____   cling   drench   strap

6. bench - e + u = _____   link   stuck   mend

7. swim - i + a = _____   plant   mint   hunt

8. cluck - u + i = _____   wrap   grin   ox

Lesson 1.13 Long Vowels

A vowel can make a long sound when followed by a consonant and silent **e**, as in r**a**k**e**, t**i**m**e**, and h**u**g**e**. Sometimes, this pattern is called **VCe**, which stands for vowel+consonant+silent e. The silent **e** makes the vowel say its name.

The letters **o** and **u** can also make a long sound when followed only by silent **e**, as in t**o**e and d**u**e.

Add silent **e** to each word and then write the new word on the line. Draw a line to match each new word to a rhyming word in the second column.

1. scrap + e = _____   fume

2. twin + e = _____   drape

3. plum + e = _____   waste

4. rod + e = _____   code

5. past + e = _____   spine

Read the meanings below. On the line, write the word from the box that matches each meaning.

lake	spine	doe	whale	true

1. _____ a female deer

2. _____ the opposite of false

3. _____ a large body of water

4. _____ the backbone

5. _____ a huge mammal that lives in the ocean

Lesson 1.13 Long Vowels

Read the paragraphs below. Write the bold words under the correct headings.

We decided to hold our charity car wash on a **nice** day in **June**. We wanted to raise money for a group that helps homeless families. Mr. Glaser asked the class to **vote**, and a car wash was the most popular choice.

We **made** a bunch of colorful signs in art class last week. The night before the big day, Dad took **Kate**, Cristofer, **Joe**, and me on a **ride** around town to post the signs. On the morning of the car wash, the sky was **blue** and the sun **shone** brightly. We had decided that ten dollars was a fair **price** for a wash. We used a **hose** to clean the dirt and **grime** from our customers' cars. We used old towels to **wipe** down each car and polish the **chrome** to a **shine**.

By late afternoon, we were ready to wrap things up for the day. **Luke** decided to play a joke on Danita. He turned the hose on her, which started a **huge** water fight. Once everything was cleaned up, we **ate** a quick snack and counted our **pile** of money. We had earned 180 dollars for our charity. We all decided to set a **date** for next year's car wash.

Long **a**	Long **i**	Long **o**	Long **u**
_____	_____	_____	_____
_____	_____	_____	_____
_____	_____	_____	_____
_____	_____	_____	_____
	_____	_____	
	_____		
	_____		

Review Short and Long Vowels

Read each word in bold below. Underline the word beside it that has the same long or short vowel sound.

1. **shake**	spit	space	whack
2. **plump**	fox	cute	junk
3. **flop**	knock	close	chest
4. **stripe**	whip	ask	wide
5. **bone**	those	dress	fox
6. **fringe**	stride	limp	desk
7. **hatch**	west	wrap	state

Look at each picture below. On the first line, write the word that names the picture. On the second line, write a word that has the same vowel sound.

 _____
_____

 _____
_____

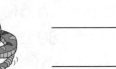 _____
_____

 _____
_____

 _____
_____

 _____
_____

Review Short and Long Vowels

Read the experiment below. In the space next to the words in bold, write the long or short vowel sound you hear.

<u>Volcano **Blast** _____</u>

- $\frac{1}{4}$ **cup** _____ baking soda
- $\frac{1}{2}$ cup water
- $\frac{1}{2}$ cup vinegar
- 8 **drops** _____ **dish** _____ soap

- dirt, **sand** _____, or soil
- a **plastic** _____ cup
- a measuring cup

1. Find a place to work where it is okay to **make** _____ a **mess** _____. Make a mound or **dome** _____ out of the dirt or sand.

2. **Use** _____ your hand to **poke** _____ a **hole** _____ in the **top** _____ of the volcano. **Fit** _____ the cup into the hole. **Press** _____ it down to **hide** _____ it.

3. **Put** _____ the baking soda into the can. In the measuring cup, **mix** _____ the water, vinegar, and soap.

4. **When** _____ you are ready for your volcano to erupt, **just** _____ pour the liquid mixture into the can of baking soda.

What causes the eruption? When the baking soda and vinegar combine, a chemical reaction **takes** _____ place and a **gas** _____ is created. The gas is what makes the **fizz** _____ or bubbles you see.

Lesson 1.14 Vowel Sounds (ai, ay, ei, ey)

The letters **ai**, **ay**, **ei**, and **ey** can make the long **a** sound you hear in paid, tray, weigh, and hey.

Read the words below. Underline the word in each set that does not have a long **a** sound.

1.	braid	quail	pass	beige
2.	reindeer	catch	hey	sway
3.	branch	gray	stain	veil
4.	stingray	paint	also	decay
5.	obey	rash	reins	clay

Look at each picture below. Write the name of the picture on the first line. Then, write each word from the box under the heading that has the same long **a** spelling.

say	weigh	bait	afraid	spray	neigh	snail	eight	tray

_____   _____   _____

_____   _____   _____

_____   _____   _____

_____   _____   _____

Lesson 1.14 Vowel Sounds (ai, ay, ei, ey)

Read each sentence below. Underline the word from the pair in parentheses that has the same long **a** sound as the word in bold.

1. The human **brain** (veil, trap) weighs about three pounds.

2. An elephant's brain **weighs** (stray, bath) about 13 pounds, and a lion's brain weighs about half a pound.

3. A neuron is a nerve cell. Scientists think there **may** (hang, they) be about 100 billion neurons in the human brain.

4. Some people **say** (brand, paid) that we use only 10% of our brains, but this isn't true—we use 100%, just not all at once.

5. An adult brain is the size of a grapefruit and is pinkish **gray** (hay, slant) in color.

6. When you feel **pain** (ranch, plate), the message travels through neurons.

7. The 28 bones in your skull help your brain **stay** (freight, crack) safe.

8. The brain is divided into two **main** (snag, play) sections. The right half controls the left side of the body and vice versa.

9. Getting enough sleep is important for keeping the brain healthy. An **eight** (fact, crate) year old needs 9 to 12 hours of sleep per day (snail, scab).

10. An **x-ray** (prey, clap) can show the different parts of the brain.

Lesson 1.15 Vowel Sounds (ee, ea, ie, ey)

The letters **ee**, **ea**, **ie**, and **ey** can make the long **e** sound you hear in tree, speak, shield, and donkey.

Look at each picture. Fill in the blanks with the long **e** spelling that correctly names the picture. Then, circle the word below it that has the long **e** sound.

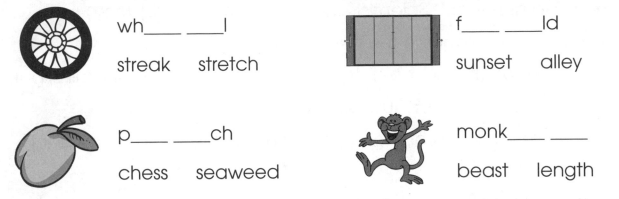

wh____ ____l

streak   stretch

f____ ____ld

sunset   alley

p____ ____ch

chess   seaweed

monk____ ____

beast   length

Read each clue. Choose the word from the box that matches the clue, and write it on the line. Circle the letters in the word that make the long **e** sound.

dream	hockey	Tennessee	niece	parakeet

1. I am a southern state. My capital is Nashville. _____

2. I am a game played in an ice rink on skates. You need a stick and a puck to play. _____

3. The son of a brother or sister is a nephew. I am the daughter of a brother or sister. _____

4. I am a small bird that is often kept as a household pet. _____

5. I am a story that your mind makes up while you sleep. _____

Lesson 1.15 Vowel Sounds (ee, ea, ie, ey)

The Morales family is going shopping. Read their lists and circle the words that have long **e** spelled **ee** and **ie**. Underline the words that have long **e** spelled **ea** and **ey**.

Romanos' Grocery	World Mart and Co.	Lincoln's
apples	birdseed	jeans for Olivia
bananas	vitamins	jacket for Marco
parsley	three rolls of paper towels	socks
tomatoes		handkerchiefs
green onions	dog treats	soccer jerseys
honey	birthday card	
peanut butter	tinfoil	
dinner rolls	sugar-free gum	
sliced turkey	beach towels	
four pieces of catfish	printer paper	
milk	bleach	
sour cream	can opener	
	tweezers	

Circle the word that has the same long vowel sound as the word in bold.

1. **belief**   slept   breeze   weigh
2. **valley**   cell   health   sweet
3. **fifteen**   wheat   quench   veil
4. **attorney**   bleed   present   they
5. **peace**   pledge   shield   neck

NAME _____

Lesson 1.16 Vowel Sounds (ind, ild, igh)

> The vowel **i** can make a long sound when followed by **nd, ld**, or **gh**, as in kind, wild, and flight.

Read the sentences below. Circle the two rhyming words with the long **i** sound in each sentence.

1. "Don't forget, these are wild animals," the zookeeper told the child.
2. Dad never has to remind Carter to rewind the videotapes.
3. Ethan might have stage fright when he sees how many people are here.
4. Did you find any lemon rind we could add to the muffin batter?
5. Bethany can't sleep at night without a light.
6. There was a wild storm yesterday, but the weather is mild today.

Read each sentence and the set of words below it. Underline the word that has the same long vowel sound as the word in bold.

1. Mom says Dylan has a one-track **mind**.

   tripped   sight   rain

2. As a **child**, he loved taking things apart and putting them back together.

   permit   squint   shine

3. When he was only four, he repaired a broken **flashlight** and radio.

   unkind   bliss   forgive

4. If Dylan can't **find** a part he needs, he can usually use something else.

   weigh   wild   wink

Lesson 1.16 Vowel Sounds (ind, ild, igh)

Unscramble the letters in bold to form a word with the long **i** sound that makes sense in the sentence. Write the word on the line.

1. _____ The opposite of in front of is **inbhed**.

2. _____ Nate stays up until **ghmniidt** on New Year's Eve.

3. _____ Remember to **ndwi** the grandfather clock every few days so that it doesn't stop ticking.

4. _____ How **hgih** can you count in Spanish?

5. _____ Are those peppers spicy or **mldi**?

6. _____ Our cat has been **nbild** in one eye since birth.

7. _____ Grandpa and Noah picked **dliw** blueberries and made a pie.

8. _____ **nduniw** the string from the yo-yo.

Write each word from the box under the heading that has the same long **i** spelling.

blindly	starlight	kindest	uptight	winding
flight	stepchild	delight	grind	wilder

tonight	mild	behind
_____	_____	_____
_____	_____	_____
_____	_____	_____

Lesson 1.17 Vowel Sounds (**oa**, **ow**, **ou**, **old**, **ost**)

- The letters **oa** and **ow** can make the long **o** sound you hear in float and grown.
- The vowel **o** can make a long sound when followed by **ld**, **ll**, and **st**, as in told, troll, and most.

Look at each picture. Fill in the blanks with the long **o** spelling that correctly names the picture.

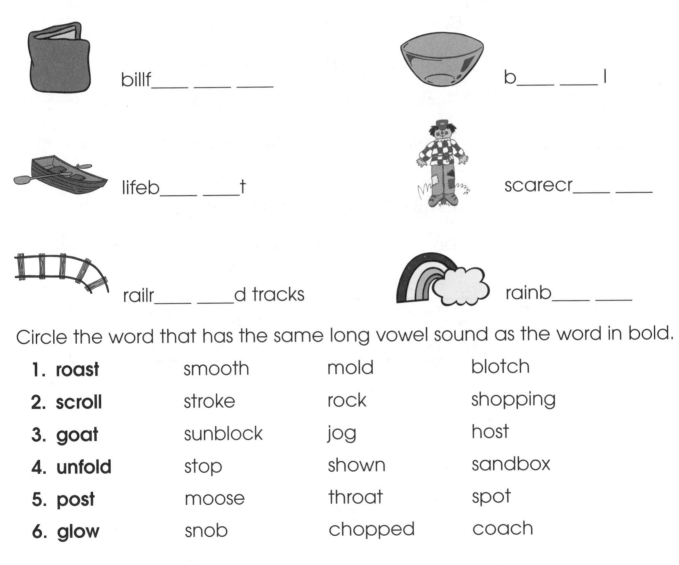

billf____ ____ ____

b____ ____ l

lifeb____ ____t

scarecr____ ____

railr____ ____d tracks

rainb____ ____

Circle the word that has the same long vowel sound as the word in bold.

1. **roast**	smooth	mold	blotch
2. **scroll**	stroke	rock	shopping
3. **goat**	sunblock	jog	host
4. **unfold**	stop	shown	sandbox
5. **post**	moose	throat	spot
6. **glow**	snob	chopped	coach

Lesson 1.17 Vowel Sounds (**oa**, **ow**, **ou**, **old**, **ost**)

On the line, write the word in parentheses that best completes each sentence below. Circle the letters that make the long **o** sound in the word.

1. On a gray, wet day, Mr. Watkins and his wife took a

    _____ by the river. (stroll, school)

2. They stopped in surprise when they heard a _____

    coming from the water. (goose, groan)

3. A man was _____ on a piece of driftwood in the chilly

    water! (couch, floating)

4. Mr. Watkins ran back to his car for a piece of rope to

    _____ the man to safety. (block, tow)

5. "I _____ gave up thinking someone would spot me,"

    said the man, huddled in Mrs. Watkins' jacket. (almost, chop)

6. "What were you doing in the water on such a _____

    day?" asked Mrs. Watkins. (pool, cold)

7. "I took my _____ out to test the new oars I just bought,"

    he replied. (rowboat, frog)

8. "A tree limb snapped and cracked my boat," he added. He

    _____ the Watkins where the branch had injured his leg.

    (showed, hound)

9. "I guess today was my lucky day," he _____ his rescuers.

    (pond, told)

Review Vowel Sounds

- **Ai, ay, ei**, and **ey** can make the long **a** sound. (trail, stay, eight, they)
- **Ee, ea, ie**, and **ey** can make the long **e** sound. (screen, neat, chief, hockey)
- The letter **i** can make a long sound when followed by **nd, ld**, or **gh**. (mind, wild, sigh)
- The letter **o** can make a long sound when followed by **ld, ll**, and **st**. (hold, roll, post)
- The letters **oa** and **ow** can make the long **o** sound. (toad, snow)

Look at the pictures below. On the first line, write the word that names each picture. On the second line, write the word from the box that rhymes with it.

mail	contain	note	degree

_____

_____

_____

_____

_____

_____

_____

_____

Read each set of words below. Underline the words that have the same long vowel sound.

1. bleach   obey   between   unkind
2. spray   weigh   shield   snow
3. neigh   blind   midnight   niece
4. mold   foam   dropped   moist

Review Vowel Sounds

Read the paragraphs below. On the line next to the words in bold, write the long vowel sound you hear (**a**, **e**, **i**, or **o**) when you say the word to yourself.

Serena Williams started **playing** _____ tennis as a very young **child** _____. By the time she was five years **old** _____, she and her older sister, Venus, were already entering tournaments. When Serena was **fourteen** _____, she went professional. **Most** _____ players don't have to compete against members of their family, but Serena and Venus have played **each** _____ other many times.

In 1999, Serena **defeated** _____ the world's top female player, Martina Hingis. She played **straight** _____ sets and won her first "grand slam title" at the U.S. Open. Other grand slam titles are the Australian Open, the French Open, and Wimbledon. Serena has won seven titles playing singles. She and her sister have won all four grand slam titles playing doubles as a **team** _____. **They** _____ are the first sisters to do this since the late 1800s. They were also the first sisters to ever **hold** _____ numbers one and two in the world rankings.

Because she hurt her ankle and **knee** _____, Serena has had to take a break from tennis for a while. But fans will continue to **keep** _____ their eyes on Serena Williams. She is sure to have a **bright** _____ future--in the world of sports and in whatever other challenges she chooses.

Lesson 1.18 Vowel Sounds (oo, ew, ou, ui)

- The letters **oo**, **ew**, **ou**, and **ui** can all make the /oo/ sound you hear in words like goose, flew, group, and bruise.
- The letters **oo** can also make the sound you hear in good and shook.

On the first line, write the word that names the picture. Then, write each word from the box under the heading that has the same vowel sound and is spelled the same way..

| suit zoo classroom cashew hood threw bruise overlook |

_____   _____   _____   _____

_____   _____   _____   _____

_____   _____   _____   _____

Read the paragraphs below. Circle the 13 words that have the /oo/ sound. Underline the 3 words that have the vowel sound you hear in look.

One afternoon, the Lyle family entered a contest and won a four-day cruise. They packed their suitcases and flew to Florida. When they arrived, there were groups of bright balloons all around the ship's deck. Jenna and Will couldn't wait to put on their bathing suits and hop in the pool.

Just past noon, the ship's whistle blew, and the Lyles were on their way. They had a light lunch of soup, sandwiches, fruit, and fresh juice. Will stretched out on his towel with a good book while Jenna went swimming. Mrs. Lyle grinned. "It looks like four days won't be long enough for any of us!"

Lesson 1.18 Vowel Sounds (**oo, ew, ou, ui**)

Read the clues below. Underline the word that best matches each clue.
Then, circle the letters that make the /oo/ sound in that word.

1. I am eaten like a vegetable, but I am actually a type of fungus.

   stoop   mushroom   juice

2. I am a group of people who work together on a boat or a plane.

   crew   school   caboose

3. I am a black-and-blue mark on your skin when you get hurt.

   goose   review   bruise

4. I am a type of soup that usually contains chunks of meat and vegetables.

   stew   scoop   group

5. I am a type of formal clothing. I include a jacket and pants or a skirt.

   scoot   suit   hook

6. I am an animal that carries my baby in a pouch. I live in Australia.

   cartoon   kangaroo   raccoon

7. I am a kind of bird.

   zoom   group   goose

8. I am a homograph for, or a word that sounds the same as, threw.

   through   tool   though

9. I am the material that covers a caterpillar before it turns into a butterfly.

   balloon   soup   cocoon

10. I am a type of soap used for washing hair.

   shampoo   drool   youth

Lesson 1.19 Vowel Sounds (**au, aw, al, all**)

- The letters **au** can make the sound you hear in taught.
- The letters **aw** can make the sound you hear in straw.
- When the vowel **a** is followed by **l** or **ll**, as in chalk or ball, it makes the same sound as **au** and **aw** do.

Make a check mark ✓ on the line next to the word that has the same vowel sound as the word in bold.

1. Are you going to listen to the **author**, Nelly Maddox, speak at the library?

   _____ apple   _____ sauce   _____ cheat

2. She is going to **talk** about her childhood and her writing.

   _____ claw   _____ clap   _____ waste

3. Ms. Maddox was born in **Australia**, but today she lives in London.

   _____ cast   _____ salt   _____ sand

4. She will be signing **autographs** from 3:00 until 5:30.

   _____ lake   _____ hall   _____ tails

5. She loved to **draw** as a little girl and illustrates all her picture books.

   _____ bang   _____ wait   _____ caught

6. Ms. Maddox's first book for teens was called **Oddball** Summer.

   _____ trash   _____ road   _____ lawn

7. It was based on her memories of feeling **awkward** as a teenager.

   _____ sail   _____ malt   _____ thank

8. Ms. Maddox's **daughter**, Amelia, likes to read and play soccer.

   _____ hawk   _____ unwrap   _____ grasp

Lesson 1.19 Vowel Sounds (au, aw, al, all)

Read each clue. Fill in the letters to complete the word that matches the clue.

1. the season that follows summer   ____ ____ tumn

2. a long, skinny tube used for drinking liquid   str____ ____

3. a type of meat that is often eaten for breakfast   s____ ____ sage

4. many stores grouped together in one place   m____ ____ ____

5. the past tense of the word catch   c____ ____ ght

6. to try out for a part in a play   ____ ____ dition

Read the sentences below. Underline the word from the pair in parentheses that best completes each sentence.

1. Harry Truman was a (southpaw, seesaw), which means he was left-handed.

2. Ulysses S. Grant brought the first professional (baseball, rainfall) team to the White House.

3. Every spring, the famous Egg (Salt, Roll) takes place on the White House (chalk, lawn).

4. George W. Bush watched the (caution, launch) of the space shuttle Discovery from the Oval Office in 2005.

5. John F. Kennedy's (autograph, jigsaw) can be worth thousands of dollars.

6. Every two years, about 650 bills are passed by Congress and signed into (law, fault) by the president.

7. The job of the Secret Service is to protect the president from an (auto, assault).

Lesson 1.20 Vowel Diphthongs (oi, oy)

A **diphthong** (pronounced dip thong) is a combination of two vowel sounds that come together and create a new sound.
- The diphthong **oi**, as in spoil, and **oy**, as in joy, make the same sound.

Underline the words in each set that have the same vowel sound.

1. avoid	frog	destroy	belong
2. stomp	globe	appoint	royal
3. coast	spoil	voyage	plot
4. moist	Floyd	those	joint
5. below	toilet	employ	potluck
6. pinpoint	throne	foil	annoy

Complete each sentence below with a word from the box. Then, circle the diphthong in the word.

spoiled	corduroy	oysters	foil	oink	cowboy

1. _____ is the sound a pig makes.

2. Clothes can be made out of a soft type of material called

   _____.

3. _____ are a type of shellfish that are often served at seafood restaurants.

4. A _____ is a person who cares for cattle on a ranch.

5. Something that is rotten is _____.

6. A shiny silver material used for covering food is called

   _____.

Lesson 1.20 Vowel Diphthongs (oi, oy)

Read each sentence below. Underline the word that has the same diphthong as the word in parentheses.

1. The pilot's voice was hard to hear through the headset. (broil)
2. There was a lot of noise and confusion in the background. (spoil)
3. "I knew our voyage would be dangerous, but I didn't expect anything like this," Captain Markham told command central. (annoy)
4. "Can you see the asteroid from your present location?" asked Daniela Pierce. (joint)
5. "It's enormous, and I'm worried it will be hard to avoid!" exclaimed the captain. (foil)
6. "I'm lucky to have a loyal crew on board with me," he added. (soybean)
7. "This may be your last chance to get out before the spacecraft is destroyed," warned Daniela. (employ)
8. "That isn't a choice," replied Captain Markham. (point)
9. Suddenly, Daniela could hear the sounds of people rejoicing on the spacecraft. (boil)
10. She smiled and took off her headphones. Nothing could change the joy and relief she felt at that moment. (Roy)

Lesson 1.21 More Vowel Diphthongs (ou, ow)

> The diphthong **ou**, as in found, and **ow**, as in growl, make the same sound.

Read each sentence below. Rewrite the sentence, replacing each picture with a word that contains the diphthong **ou** or **ow**.

1. Eva's grandma travels  for the winter.

   _____

2. The  made balloon animals at the birthday party.

   _____

3. Who spilled grape juice all over the ?

   _____

4. We need to find a 👑 to complete Jake's costume.

   _____

5. Oscar climbed to the top of the 🗼 and looked for ships.

   _____

6. Stratus and cumulus are different types of ☁.

   _____

Lesson 1.21 More Vowel Diphthongs (**ou**, **ow**)

Read the paragraphs below. Circle the 11 words that contain the /ow/ sound spelled **ou**. Underline the five words that have the /ow/ sound spelled **ow**. You do not need to mark the same word more than once.

You'll find milk in the refrigerator of almost every house in America. People drink it, pour it on their cereal, and cook with it. Do you know where milk comes from? How does it get from a cow to your kitchen table?

Dairy farms are located all around the country, but many are found in the Midwest. Farmers feed cows a mixture of hay, barley, corn, cottonseed, grasses, and grocery store leftovers. A single cow eats as much as 80 pounds a day! Cows drink a large amount of water too—about 40 gallons daily.

A mother cow produces around eight gallons of milk a day. In the past, people milked by hand. The farmer would crouch on the ground or sit on a stool beside the cow. He or she would squeeze out milk into pails from the cow's udders. Today, cows go to a milking parlor where they are hooked up to a powerful machine. It cools the milk and pumps it into big storage containers. This is faster and easier than milking by hand. Using the machines allows farmers to milk more cows.

The milk is picked up every day by a special truck. The metal tanks store the milk and keep it cool as it travels to a processing plant. Now the milk is heated to kill any bacteria. It is put into bottles and cartons and shipped to grocery stores all across the nation. Where would we be without dairy farmers? There is no doubt that they are a very important part of the food industry.

Review Vowel Sounds and Diphthongs

- **Oo, ew, ou,** and **ui** can make the /oo/ sound, as in bloom, flew, youth, and suit. **Oo** can also make the sound you hear in wood and hook.
- **Au** and **aw** can make the same vowel sound, as in caught and straw. When **a** is followed by **l** or **ll**, as in walk or tall, it makes the /aw/ sound, too.

Read the clues below. Choose the word from the box that matches each clue and write it in the puzzle.

cashew	juice	hook	neighborhood	August	chalk	soup	claw

Across
2. liquid food eaten with a spoon
3. a blackboard writing tool
6. a group of houses near one another
7. the sharp nail of an animal

Down
1. the liquid of a fruit
3. a type of nut
4. the month that follows July
5. a metal piece used to catch fish

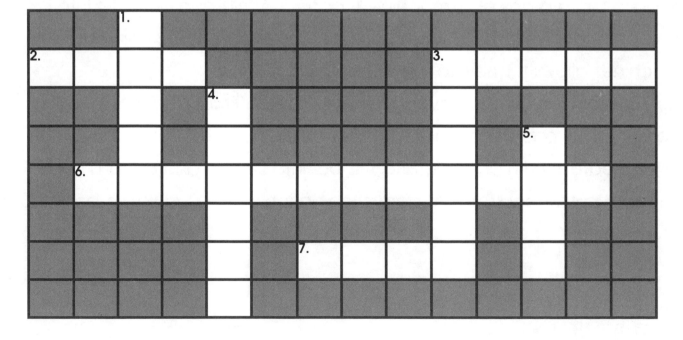

Review Vowel Sounds and Diphthongs

Remember, a diphthong is a combination of two vowel sounds that create a new sound.
- The diphthongs **oi** and **oy** make the same sound, as in noise and loyal.
- The diphthongs **ou** and **ow** make the same sound, as in trout and power.

Read the sentences below. On the line, write the word from the box that best completes each sentence. Then, circle the diphthong in the word.

| proud | firehouse | loyal | pound | choice |

1. The firefighters decided they needed a dog at the _____.

2. Captain Fox said they should go to the _____ to find a dog who needed a good home.

3. It didn't take long for them to make their _____.

4. The captain was _____ to say that Dixie chose Squad 615.

5. He knew she would be a good friend and a _____ dog.

Read each clue below. Fill in the blanks to form a word that matches the clue.

1. the last car of a train, often painted red   cab____ ____se

2. the opposite of short   t____ ____ ____

3. a trip or a journey   v____ ____age

4. a young deer   f____ ____n

5. clothes that need to be washed   l____ ____ndry

6. the color of chocolate   br____ ____n

Lesson 1.22 The Schwa Sound

The vowels **a**, **e**, **i**, **o**, and **u** can all make the **schwa sound**. It is the /uh/ sound you hear at the beginning of the word about and at the end of the word label. The symbol that stands for the schwa sound (ə) looks like an upside-down **e**. In each word below, the vowel that makes the schwa sound is in bold.

around   sev**e**n   April   comm**o**n   circ**u**s

Read the sentences below. For each word in bold, circle the vowel that makes the schwa sound.

1. An **atlas** is a book that contains maps.

2. You can find a map of **China** on page 42.

3. On which page did you find information about the Grand **Canyon**?

4. We are going to drive across the country in a **rental** car.

5. Grandpa Louis keeps a **travel** log of all the places he has been.

6. Use a **pencil** to jot down these directions.

7. Let's plan to stop at the **cactus** garden in New Mexico.

Read each clue and the word beside it. Replace the schwa with a vowel to spell the word that matches the clue. Write the word on the line.

1. an underground passage   tunnəl   _____

2. a piece of farm equipment   tractər   _____

3. last   finəl   _____

4. by oneself   əlone   _____

5. causing pain or suffering   cruəl   _____

6. the way a horse runs   galləp   _____

Lesson 1.22 The Schwa Sound

Look at each picture below. On the line, write the word from the box that names the picture. Circle the vowel that makes the schwa sound.

Hint: Some words may have more than one schwa sound.

| elephant | pencil | lemon | towel | banana | circus |

_____ _____ _____

_____ _____ _____

Read the words below. Circle the word in each set that contains the schwa sound. If you are not sure, try saying the words out loud to yourself.

1. press   thick   legal
2. canoe   blond   drank
3. begin   belt   children
4. classical   chalkboard   spring
5. crept   even   cube
6. knock   length   possum
7. band   often   ditch

Lesson 1.22 The Schwa Sound

The **schwa sound** is usually found in unstressed syllables. When you divide a word into syllables, one syllable is often stressed. In the word a·bove', the second syllable is stressed. The first syllable has the schwa sound.

Here are some other words that have the schwa sound. The vowel that makes the schwa sound is in bold. Notice how the schwa sound is in the unstressed syllable in each word below.

a·round'   len'·til   sev'·en   pi'·lot   wish'·ful

Read the sentences below. For each word in bold, circle the unstressed syllable and underline the vowel that makes the schwa sound.

Ex.: Grandma made **pas·ta** for dinner.

1. When Max turned **sev·en**, he had his birthday party at the zoo.

2. Max's favorite part of the zoo is the **Ser·pent** House.

3. He knows all the snakes by their **com·mon** names.

4. Greenbrook Zoo keeps **a·bout** 500 snakes at the Serpent House.

5. Max's friends **a·gree** that snakes are the most interesting reptiles.

6. The zookeeper feeds the snakes small **mam·mals**, like mice and rats.

7. Snakes can **o·pen** their mouths wide enough to eat animals that seem much too large for them.

8. Max was surprised to learn that some snakes have sensors between their eyes and **nos·trils** that allow them to "see" the heat of another animal.

Lesson 1.22 The Schwa Sound

Many words that end in **le** make the schwa sound.

dimple (dimpəl)   ripple (rippəl)   pickle (pickəl)   castle (castəl)

Choose the word from the box that matches each clue and write it on the line. Then, find the word in the word search puzzle and circle it.

maple   freckle   marble   purple   castle   simple   beagle   apple

1. a sweet, crispy, red or green fruit   _____

2. a small glass ball used in children's games   _____

3. a color made by mixing red and blue   _____

4. a breed of hound dog   _____

5. a small, light brown spot on the skin,

   especially on the face   _____

6. easy; the opposite of difficult   _____

7. a type of sweet syrup   _____

8. a home for royalty   _____

f	p	u	r	p	l	e	h	k	b	i
c	v	e	f	r	e	c	k	l	e	v
a	m	a	r	b	l	e	j	r	a	s
s	a	f	g	j	u	y	p	w	g	o
t	p	f	d	a	j	a	p	p	l	e
l	l	z	d	s	i	m	p	l	e	u
e	e	u	d	m	a	a	e	w	k	l

Lesson 1.23 The Sounds of y

- At the beginning of a word, **y** can make the sound you hear in yell.
- The letter **y** can make the long **i** sound at the end of a word, as in spy and cry.
- The letter **y** can make the long **e** sound at the end of a word, as in heavy.
- In the middle of a word, **y** can make the short **i** sound, as in gym or the long **i** sound, as in style.

Read each sentence. Circle the word below the sentence that has the same sound of **y** as the word in bold.

1. **Butterfly** World, in Coconut Creek, Florida, is the largest butterfly house.

   system   supply   yank

2. Thousands of different **types** of butterflies live there.

   python   yes   shiny

3. There are several outdoor gardens where the butterflies fly **freely**.

   why   yellow   scary

4. The butterflies come from **many** places around the world.

   lying   easy   nylon

5. Be sure not to miss seeing the Jewels of the **Sky** Hummingbird exhibit.

   shy   mystery   carry

6. Would **you** like to learn how to start your own butterfly garden?

   yogurt   celery   apply

7. The life span of a **typical** butterfly may be only a couple of weeks.

   sly   myth   yesterday

Lesson 1.23 The Sounds of y

Read each set of words below. Write **y**, short **i**, long **i**, or long **e** on the line to show what sound the letter **y** makes in the words in the set.

1. _____ crazy   softly   party

2. _____ gym   system   Egypt

3. _____ shy   lying   dry

4. _____ quickly fairy   puppy

5. _____ yacht   yell   yowl

Read the paragraphs below. Listen to the sound the **y** makes in the words in bold. Then, write each word beside the correct heading.

    Yodeling is a form of singing. A **yodeler** moves his or her voice **quickly** back and forth between high and low sounds. Yodeling might have begun as a way for shepherds to communicate. But different **styles** of yodeling are found in **many** other cultures, too, **especially** near mountains. Yodeling is found in China, as well as among the **pygmies** of Africa and the native people of Australia. In America, yodeling can be heard in the **rhythms** of **country** and bluegrass music. Experts say that the best places to yodel are places where there is an echo. That way, **you** will always hear a **reply**.

long **e**: _____ _____ _____

_____

long **i**: _____ _____

short **i**: _____ _____

y: _____ _____ _____

Lesson 1.24 R-Controlled Vowels (ar, er, ir, or, ur)

When the letter **r** follows a vowel, it can change the vowel's sound.
- The letters **ar** make the sound you hear in park.
- The letters **or** make the sound you hear in sports.
- The letters **er**, **ir**, and **ur** can all make the same sound, as in verb, whirl, and hurt.

Read each sentence below. On the line, write a word that contains an **r**-controlled vowel and names the picture.

1. Mr. Robards asked the students to sit in a ⬭. _____

2. Annie found a 🐢 in the valley last Saturday. _____

3. Has anyone ever spotted a 🦈 at this beach? _____

4. Dad is grilling some 🌽 to go with the burgers. _____

5. Did you get a ✉️ from Steven? _____

6. Aunt Kimiko knitted Jess a 🧣 . _____

7. The 🐴 stamped his feet and whinnied when he saw the apples. _____

8. Sophie came in 🎖️ in the race. _____

Lesson 1.24 R-Controlled Vowels (ar, er, ir, or, ur)

Read each word in column 1. Write the letter of the definition on the line beside the word.

1. third _____		**a.** food usually served at Thanksgiving
2. verb _____		**b.** a musical instrument
3. thorn _____		**c.** comes between second and fourth
4. guitar _____		**d.** a part of speech; an action word
5. turkey _____		**e.** a sharp point on the stem of a plant

Read the paragraphs below. Circle the five words that have an **ar** or **or** sound. Underline the 11 words that have an **er**, **ir**, or **ur** sound. Do not mark the same word more than once.

Daniel Sullivan was the first person to be known as a horse whisperer. During the 1800s, he became famous in England for helping horses that no one else could help. Some horses were violent. Others had been abused. Daniel was able to calm the horses. They seemed to know they could trust him. Daniel taught two other men the art of horse whispering. Both men wrote books, and more and more people learned about helping troubled horses.

Can you guess how horse whispering got its name? The trainers stand face to face with their horses. People who observed this thought the trainer must be whispering something special to the horse. Actually, horse whisperers just know a lot about horses. They understand these animals better than anyone. It is hard work, and it takes a lot of patience. But most horse whisperers wouldn't dream of doing anything else.

Lesson 1.25 More R-Controlled Vowels (air, are, ear, eer)

- The letters **air** and **are** can make the same sound, as in fair and care.
- The letters **ear** and **eer** can make the same sound, as in fear and deer. **Ear** can also make the sound you hear in bear.

Look at each picture. On the line, write the word from the box that names the picture. Then, circle the rhyming word below it.

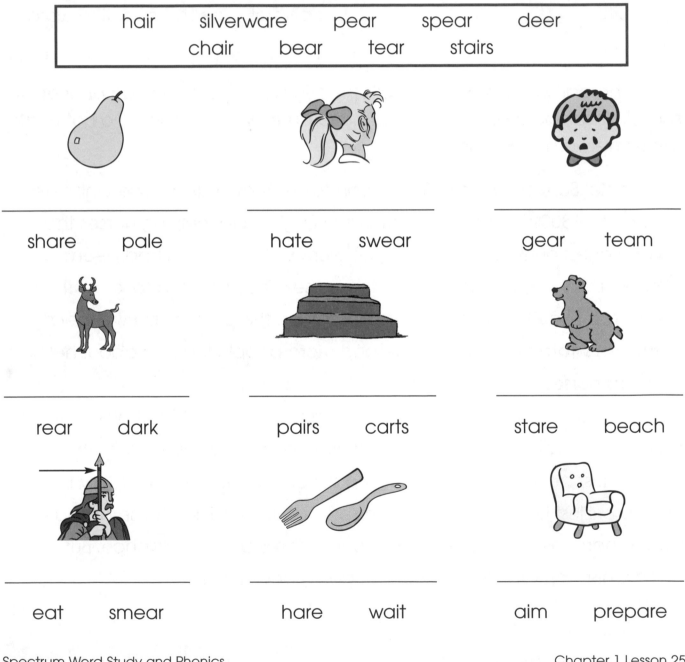

| hair | silverware | pear | spear | deer |
| chair | bear | tear | stairs | |

share   pale

hate   swear

gear   team

rear   dark

pairs   carts

stare   beach

eat   smear

hare   wait

aim   prepare

Lesson 1.25 More **R**-Controlled Vowels (**air, are, ear, eer**)

Read the paragraphs below. Underline the word from the pair in parentheses that best completes each sentence.

Locks of Love is a very special group located in Florida. Treatments for some illnesses can cause children to lose their (square, hair). Locks of Love lets people donate hair that can be made into wigs for these children. Whenever they (swear, wear) their wigs, the children are (aware, beware) that someone they've never even met (cares, glares) about them.

The hair can be any color. It can be straight or curly. Locks of Love just asks that the donations be at least 10 inches long and that people (prepare, declare) by washing their hair before it is cut. Some salons will even cut hair for free if they know it will be donated.

Although it takes (steers, years) to grow (clear, nearly) a foot of hair, hundreds of people (volunteer, appear). Most of the donations come from kids who (hear, fear) about the group and decide to help. If you would like to (blare, share) your hair or learn more about this group, visit their web site.

Read each set of words below. Circle the word that has the same **r**-controlled vowel sound as the word in bold.

1. **rare**	career	gear	spare
2. **peer**	engineer	nightmare	fare
3. **smear**	pear	dear	affair
4. **flair**	despair	appear	deer
5. **sneer**	reindeer	flare	repair

Review Schwa, the Sounds of **y**, and **R**-Controlled Vowels

> • The vowels **a**, **e**, **i**, **o**, and **u** can all make the **schwa sound** (/ə/) in unstressed syllables: **a**·wake', hap'·p**e**n, nos'·tr**i**l, meth'·**o**d, joy'·f**u**l.
> • Many words that end in **le**, like wiggle (wiggəl), also make the /ə/ sound.

Read each definition and the pronunciation beside it. On the line, write the word.

1. clapping made by a group   əp·plause'   _____

2. a story that teaches a lesson   fa'·bəl   _____

3. a sour yellow fruit   lem'·ən   _____

4. a coin worth five cents   nick'·əl   _____

5. a small paddle boat   cə·noe'   _____

The letter **y** can stand for several different sounds: the /y/ sound (yes), the long **i** sound (try), the long **e** sound (happy), and the short **i** sound (gym).

Read the sentences below. Listen to the sound the **y** makes in each word in bold. Write the sound (**y**, short **i**, long **i**, or long **e**) on the line.

1. **My** _____ aunt is planning to take a trip next **July** _____.

2. She spent **many** _____ **years** _____ learning about the pyramids.

3. She will **fly** _____ to **Egypt** _____ and stay with a **family** _____ for a month.

4. Aunt **Kelly** _____ loves the **mysteries** _____ of the pyramids.

5. I may be too **young** _____ to travel with Aunt Kelly right now, but I'd like to see the world **myself** _____ one day.

Review Schwa, the Sounds of **y**, and **R**-Controlled Vowels

When the letter **r** follows a vowel, it can change the vowel's sound.
- The letters **ar** make the sound you hear in farm.
- The letters **or** make the sound you hear in snore.
- **Er, ir**, and **ur** make the same sound, as in germ, birth, and fur.
- **Air, are**, and **ear** can make the same sound, as in pair, dare, and wear.
- **Ear** and **eer** can make the same sound, as in hear and steer.

Read each word in bold below. On the line, write the letter of the word beside it that has the same **r**-controlled vowel sound.

1. _____ **arch**   **a.** shear   **b.** merge   **c.** smart

2. _____ **chirp**   **a.** cork   **b.** surf   **c.** sneer

3. _____ **spare**   **a.** wear   **b.** porch   **c.** swirl

4. _____ **nerve**   **a.** yarn   **b.** near   **c.** dirt

5. _____ **clear**   **a.** curve   **b.** career   **c.** pear

6. _____ **fort**   **a.** sworn   **b.** stern   **c.** volunteer

Read the sentences below, and circle the words that have **r**-controlled vowels. The number in parentheses will tell you how many words you should find.

1. Monet was an artist who painted outdoors and used bright colors. (3)

2. Mary Cassatt was a painter at a time when few women had careers. (2)

3. Georgia O'Keeffe's family urged her to prepare for life as an artist at a young age. (5)

4. Norman Rockwell painted hundreds of magazine covers during his life. (3)

Lesson 2.1 Base Words and Endings (-ed, -ing)

A **base word** is a word without endings added to it.
- If a base word has a short vowel sound and ends in a consonant, double the consonant before adding **ed** or **ing**.
  drag, dra**gg**ed, dra**gg**ing
- If a base word ends with **e**, drop the **e** before adding **ed** or **ing**.
  move, moved, moving
- If a base word ends with **y**, change the **y** to **i** before adding **ed**. Do not change the **y** before adding **ing**.
  hurry, hurr**i**ed, hurr**y**ing

On the line, write the base word for each word in bold.

1. On the day of the championship, Ben **discovered** _____ that his lucky baseball mitt was **missing** _____.

2. "I'm **worried** _____ I won't find my mitt in time for the game!" **exclaimed** _____ Ben.

3. "It could be **buried** _____ in your closet," **suggested** _____ Dad. "Have you **searched** _____ in there yet?" he asked.

4. Ben **nodded** _____. "I'm not **quitting** _____ until it's time to leave for the game, though. It has to be somewhere."

5. Just then, Jasper **trotted** _____ into the kitchen, wagging his tail and **carrying** _____ Ben's worn, **creased** _____ mitt.

Lesson 2.1 Base Words and Endings (-ed, -ing)

Fill in the blanks in the chart below.

Base Word	Add -ed	Add -ing
carry	_____	_____
_____	clapped	_____
_____	_____	changing
_____	spied	_____
laugh	_____	_____
_____	_____	applying
bike	_____	_____
_____	_____	shrugging

Solve each problem below. Be sure to remember the rules for adding endings. On the second line, write a sentence using your answer.

1. whisper + ed = _____

   _____

2. study + ing = _____

   _____

3. explore + ed = _____

   _____

4. spy + ed = _____

   _____

Lesson 2.2 Base Word Endings (-s, -es)

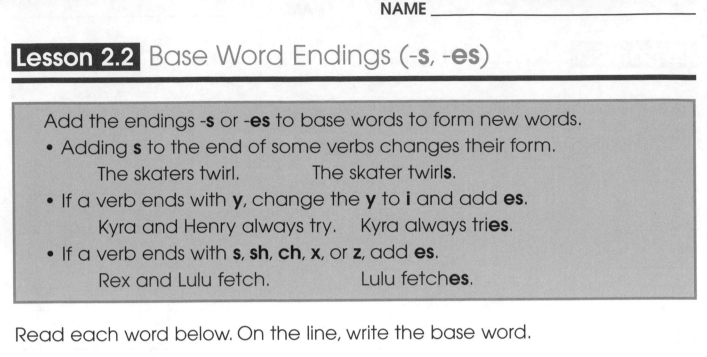

Add the endings -s or -es to base words to form new words.
- Adding **s** to the end of some verbs changes their form.
  The skaters twirl.   The skater twirl**s**.
- If a verb ends with **y**, change the **y** to **i** and add **es**.
  Kyra and Henry always try.   Kyra always tri**es**.
- If a verb ends with **s**, **sh**, **ch**, **x**, or **z**, add **es**.
  Rex and Lulu fetch.   Lulu fetch**es**.

Read each word below. On the line, write the base word.

1. touches _____

2. replies _____

3. smiles _____

4. coaxes _____

5. buzzes _____

6. cries _____

7. passes _____

8. replaces_____

Read the sentences below. Underline the word from the pair in parentheses that best completes each sentence.

1. Every Mother's Day, Anjali (cookes, cooks) breakfast for her mom.

2. She (scrambles, scrambls) eggs and (fries, frys) some pancakes.

3. Anjali (watchs, watches) the eggs closely as they cook.

4. She (mixes, mixs) the pancake ingredients carefully.

5. Finally, she (carrys, carries) the tray upstairs and (shouts, shoutes) "Happy Mother's Day!" as she (opens, openes) the door to her parents' bedroom.

Lesson 2.2 Base Word Endings (-**s**, -**es**)

Read the sentences below. Fill in the blanks with the correct form of the base words in bold.

1. Each spring, Ella and Devon **plant** their seedlings and **watch** them grow.

   Each spring, Ella _____ her seedlings and

   _____ them grow.

2. Ella and her mom **worry** that a late-spring snow will hurt the seedlings.

   Ella's mom _____ that a late-spring snow will hurt the seedlings.

3. In the summer, the Coles **pick** tomatoes, peas, and raspberries.

   In the summer, Ella _____ tomatoes, peas, and raspberries.

4. In the fall, they **harvest** pumpkins, lettuce, and butternut squash.

   In the fall, Devon _____ pumpkins, lettuce, and butternut squash.

5. Devon and Mr. Cole **rake** the leaves.

   Mr. Cole _____ the leaves.

6. The Coles **push** the wheelbarrow into the yard and grab some bags.

   Mrs. Cole _____ the wheelbarrow into the yard and grabs some bags.

Read the sets of words below. Circle the correct form of each word in bold.

1. **hike**	hikes	hiks
2. **climb**	climbs	climbes
3. **finish**	finishs	finishes
4. **bury**	buries	burys

Lesson 2.3 Comparative Endings (-**er**, -**est**)

- The endings -**er** and -**est** can be added to base words to make a comparison.

  Add **er** to mean more when comparing two things.

  neat**er** = more neat

  Add **est** to mean most when comparing three or more things.

  neat**est** = most neat

- For words that end in **e**, drop the **e** and add **er** or **est**. (nice, nic**er**, nic**est**)

- For words that end in a consonant and **y**, change the **y** to **i** before adding **er** or **est**. (busy, bus**ier**, bus**iest**)

- For words that have a short vowel sound and end in a consonant, double the consonant before adding **er** or **est**. (thin, thin**ner**, thin**nest**)

Fill in the blanks below with the correct form of the comparative word.

Base Word	Add -**er**	Add -**est**
smart	_____	_____
_____	sadder	_____
tiny	_____	_____
_____	_____	brightest
wet	_____	_____
_____	funnier	_____
quick	_____	quickest
_____	cleaner	_____
gentle	_____	_____
_____	_____	prettiest

Lesson 2.3 Comparative Endings (-**er**, -**est**)

Read the sentences below. On the line, write the correct comparative form of each word in parentheses.

1. Venus is the planet with the _____ surface. (hot)

2. Mercury has a _____ orbit than Venus. (fast)

3. Jupiter has the _____ moon of all the planets in our solar system. (large)

4. Neptune's year is _____ than Uranus's. (long)

5. The _____ star to Earth is about 25 trillion miles away. (close)

6. Venus is the _____ planet and can often be seen by the naked eye. (bright)

7. The _____ volcano in the solar system, Olympus Mons, is found on Mars. (big)

8. It is much _____ on Neptune than on Earth. Winds on Neptune can reach about 1,200 miles per hour! (windy)

Phonics Connection

Use your answers from the exercise above to answer the following question.

Two words have the hard **g** sound, and one has the soft **g** sound. Write the words on the lines. hard **g**: _____ _____

soft **g**: _____

Review Base Words and Endings

Remember these rules when adding endings to base words:

- For some base words, double the consonant before adding **ed** or **ing**. (plan, plan**ned**, plan**ning**)
- If a base word ends with **e**, drop the **e** before adding **ed** or **ing**. (live, liv**ed**, liv**ing**)
- If a base word ends with **y**, change the **y** to **i** before adding **ed** or **es**. Do not change the **y** before adding **ing**. (worry, worr**ied**, worry**ing**)
- If a word ends with **s**, **sh**, **ch**, **x**, or **z**, add **es**. (watch, watch**es**)

Solve each problem below. Remember the rules for adding endings. On the second line, write a sentence using your answer.

1. hurry + ed = _____

   _____

2. drip + ed = _____

   _____

3. carry + ing = _____

   _____

Underline the word that best completes each sentence below.

1. On Thursday nights, Mom (swimes, swims) at the YMCA.
2. Dad usually (toss's, tosses) around a ball with me in the gym.
3. He (studied, studyied) sports psychology in college.
4. Dad (clapped, claped) when I showed him some new moves.
5. When Mom (finishs, finishes) her laps, we head home.

Review Base Words and Endings

> Remember, the ending **-er** means more and is used to compare two things. The ending **-est** means most and is used to compare three or more things.
> - If a words ends in **e**, drop the **e** and add **er** or **est**. If it ends in a consonant and **y**, change the **y** to **i** before adding **er** or **est**.
>   close, clos**er**, clos**est**   heavy, heav**ier**, heav**iest**
> - For words that have a short vowel sound and end in a consonant, double the consonant before adding **er** or **est**.
>   sad, sad**der**, sad**dest**

Read the sentences below. On the line, write the comparative form of the words in parentheses.

1. The _____ snake in the world is called the black mamba. (most deadly)

2. The Komodo dragon is the world's _____ lizard. It can eat about 80% of its body's weight in just one day. (most large)

3. Even a spider moves faster than a sloth, the world's

   _____-moving land mammal. (most slow)

4. The average giraffe is three times _____ than a camel. (more tall)

5. The koala, the _____ animal, spends about 22 hours a day snoozing. (most sleepy)

6. One of the _____-looking bugs is the stick insect, which can measure more than one foot in length. (most strange)

7. At 60 feet long, the giant squid is _____ than most under sea creatures. (more big)

Lesson 2.4 Plurals

The word plural means more than one. To form the plural of most words, just add **s**.

     house, house**s**

- If a noun ends in **sh**, **ch**, **s**, or **x**, add **es**.

     bench, bench**es**

- If a noun ends with a consonant and **y**, drop the **y** and add **ies**.

     story, stor**ies**

- For some words that end in **f** or **fe**, change the **f** or **fe** to **v** and add **es**. Form the plural of other words, like roof, belief, and cliff, by adding **s**.

     life, li**ves**

Read the paragraphs below. On the line, write the plural form of each word in parentheses.

     Aleesha was packing the _____ (content) of her room. Downstairs, the _____ (glass), _____ (dish), books, and _____ (picture) had been packed. She had said good-bye to her two best _____ (friend) and all the nearby _____ (family) in the neighborhood.

     Aleesha packed her stuffed _____ (animal). She grinned when she saw the soft gray _____ (wolf) her grandpa had brought her. He often traveled west, hiking and camping in the _____ (mountain) and climbing _____ (cliff). Aleesha remembered that the new house was only _____ (minute) away from Grandpa Harry's. She took a deep breath and zipped her bag. Aleesha was ready to go.

Lesson 2.4 Plurals

Read the clues below. Choose the word from the box that matches each clue. Write the plural form of the word in the numbered spaces in the crossword puzzle.

| backpack | knife | calf | diary | candy | sandwich | planet | wish |

Across

2. a body in the solar system
6. two pieces of bread with filling between
7. a journal used for recording events
8. a piece of silverware used for cutting

Down

1. a baby cow
3. a sweet treat
4. a bag used for carrying books
5. a hope that something happens

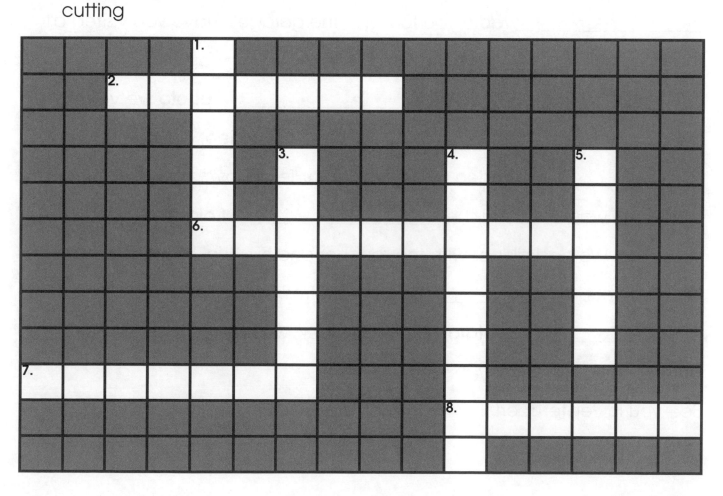

Lesson 2.4 Plurals

> - If a word ends with a vowel and the letter **o**, form the plural by adding **s**.   stereo, stereo**s**   patio, patio**s**
> - If a word ends with a consonant and **o**, form the plural by adding **es**.
>   potato, potato**es**   torpedo, torpedo**es**
> - A few words do not follow this pattern. Just add **s** to the following words to form the plural: photo, burro, auto, Eskimo, pro, piano, solo, soprano.

On the line, write the plural form of each word in bold.

Dear Jacob,

How has your summer been? Have you repaired all those old

_____ **radio** you found in the garage? Have you visited all

the _____ **zoo** in Ohio yet?

I can't wait to show you the _____ **photo** we've taken.

My aunt has shot dozens of _____ **video**. We went to

_____ **rodeo** in three different Texas towns. My favorite part

of the trip was watching the _____ **buffalo** at a ranch in

Wyoming. We had dinner with the rancher and his wife. They served us

juicy burgers, _____ **tomato** fresh from the garden, and fried

_____ **potato**. Later that week, we rode _____

burro in the Grand Canyon.

See you in September!

Cole

Lesson 2.4 Plurals

Read the clues below. On the line, write the plural form of the word from the box that matches each clue.

| shampoo | igloo | flamingo | piano | mango | zero |

1. _____ a bright pink tropical bird with long, skinny legs

2. _____ the number that equals nothing

3. _____ a dome-shaped home made of ice or snow

4. _____ an instrument that has 88 keys

5. _____ a type of soap used for washing hair

6. _____ a sweet, tropical fruit

Circle the correct plural form in each pair of words below.

1. torpedoes   torpedos

2. shampoos   shampooes

3. heros   heroes

4. patios   patioes

5. autoes   autos

6. mosquitos   mosquitoes

7. solos   soloes

Phonics Connection

One word in the second exercise has the schwa sound. Write the word on the line and circle the vowel that makes the schwa sound.

_____

Lesson 2.5 Irregular Plurals

Some plural words do not follow the patterns you have learned. You must memorize the **irregular plural** forms of these words.

child, children   foot, feet   die, dice   goose, geese   ox, oxen
woman, women   man, men   mouse, mice   tooth, teeth

The singular and plural forms of the following words are the same: deer, fish, moose, sheep, trout, salmon, wheat, series, traffic, and species.

Choose a word from the box to replace each picture in the following sentences and write it on the line.

sheep	mice	foot	children	fish

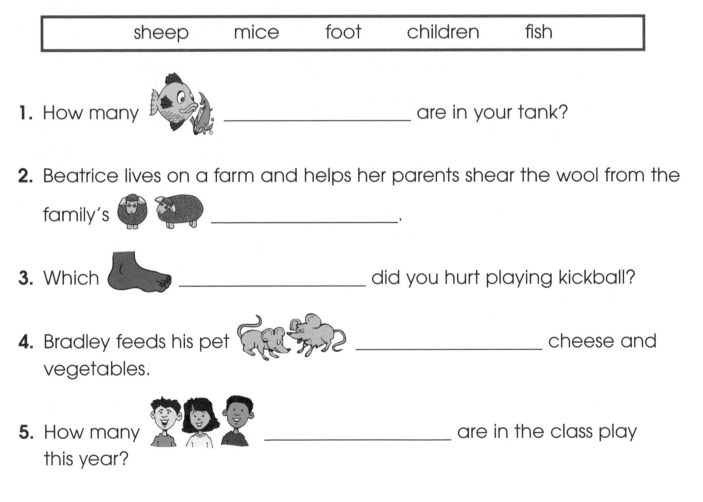

1. How many _____ are in your tank?

2. Beatrice lives on a farm and helps her parents shear the wool from the family's _____.

3. Which _____ did you hurt playing kickball?

4. Bradley feeds his pet _____ cheese and vegetables.

5. How many _____ are in the class play this year?

Lesson 2.5 Irregular Plurals

Read each sentence below. If the word in bold is spelled correctly, make a check mark on the line. If it is incorrect, write the correct form of the word on the line.

1. _____ Most **salmon** return to the place they were born to lay their eggs.

2. _____ All of the **womans** in the Mendez family went to the picnic.

3. _____ Toss the **dices** to find out how many spaces you can move.

4. _____ The vet had to pull two of Ripley's **teeth**.

5. _____ Two **gooses** and their babies waddled across the road.

6. _____ What can we do to keep the **deers** from eating the lettuce in our garden?

7. _____ The two stubborn **oxen** refused to budge.

Fill in the blanks in each item below.

1. one fish   three _____

2. one moose   a herd of _____

3. a _____   a group of children

4. one tooth   several _____

5. one _____   two dice

6. a man   120 _____

7. a _____   14 trout

Lesson 2.6 Possessives

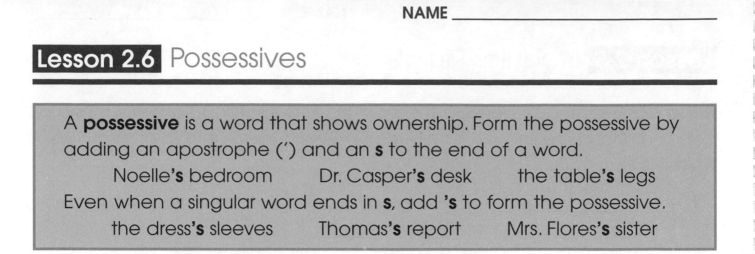

A **possessive** is a word that shows ownership. Form the possessive by adding an apostrophe (') and an **s** to the end of a word.

Noelle**'s** bedroom   Dr. Casper**'s** desk   the table**'s** legs

Even when a singular word ends in **s**, add **'s** to form the possessive.

the dress**'s** sleeves   Thomas**'s** report   Mrs. Flores**'s** sister

Look at the pictures, and read the phrases below. On the line, write the possessive form of each phrase.

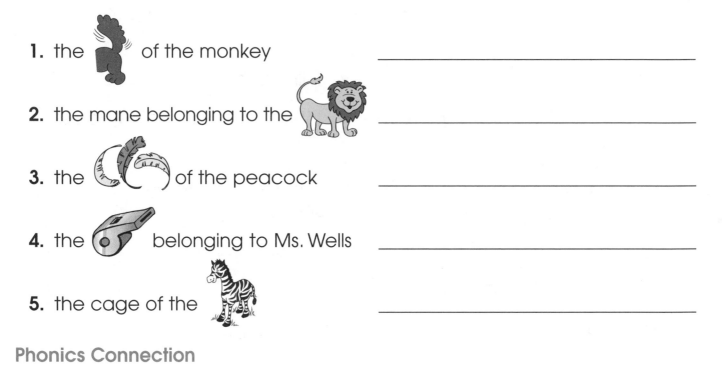

1. the 🦶 of the monkey   _____

2. the mane belonging to the 🦁   _____

3. the 🪶 of the peacock   _____

4. the 🎵 belonging to Ms. Wells   _____

5. the cage of the 🦓   _____

Phonics Connection

Find the three words above that have the long **a** sound and write them on the lines. Then, write two new words beside them with the same long **a** spellings.

_____   _____   _____

_____   _____   _____

_____   _____   _____

Lesson 2.6 Possessives

Read the paragraphs below. Find the six possessives and circle them.

   Anna Mary Robertson, better known as Grandma Moses, became an artist late in life. She had spent most of her life as a farmer's wife and a mother and only started painting in her 70s. Most of Grandma Moses's paintings were set in the country. Each paintings' colors were bright and cheerful. They showed family life in America during the first part of the 20th century.

   The more people who saw the artist's work, the more popular it became. The paintings were displayed in museums around the world. In 1949, President Truman gave Grandma Moses the Women's National Press Club Award. Although she had a late start to her career, Grandma Moses kept painting until she was nearly 100. Today, a museum's collection of folk art is not complete without a Grandma Moses original.

Read the sentences below. If the word in bold is plural, write **PL** on the line. If it is possessive, write **PO**.

1. _____ Grandma Moses's **paintings** were first noticed in a drugstore window.

2. _____ The collector bought all the paintings for just a few **dollars**.

3. _____ Grandma Moses lived to be 101 **years** old.

4. _____ This interesting **woman's** life has been written about in books, magazines, and newspapers.

Lesson 2.6 Possessives

To form a **plural possessive**, add an apostrophe (') to the end of a plural word.
> the balloon**s'** strings   the babie**s'** bottles

If a plural word does not end in **s**, add an apostrophe plus **s** ('**s**).
> the children**'s** toys   the geese**'s** eggs

Read the newspaper headlines below. The possessives in the headlines are written incorrectly. On each line, rewrite the headline with the correct form of the plural possessive.

1. Little Valley Girls's Soccer Team Wins Championship

_____

2. Experts Say Mooses' Food Source Quickly Disappearing

_____

3. Storms's High Winds Knock Out Power across Midwest

_____

4. Miners's Strike Surprises Kentucky Town

_____

Read each phrase below. On the line, write the plural possessive.

1. the wool of the sheep _____

2. the bats belonging to the players _____

3. the tickets belonging to the families _____

4. the uniforms of the men _____

5. the dog belonging to the McKenzies _____

Lesson 2.6 Possessives

Read each phrase below. If it is plural, write **PL** on the line. If it is singular possessive, write **SP**. If it is plural possessive, write **PP**.

1. _____ the strawberries' stems

2. _____ a bushel of peaches

3. _____ the plum's pit

4. _____ Mrs. Polini's fruit salad

5. _____ the mangoes and pears

6. _____ the children's fruit pizza

Read the phrases below. Circle the letter of the correct plural possessive form.

1. the party of the Gilberts

   a. the Gilberts' party   **b.** the Gilbert's party

2. the presents belonging to the people

   a. the peoples' presents   **b.** the people's presents

3. the laughter of the boys

   a. the boys's laughter   **b.** the boys' laughter

4. the barking of the dogs

   a. the dogs' barking   **b.** the dog's barking

Phonics Connection

On the lines below, list the three words with digraphs from exercise 1. Circle the digraph in each word.

_____ _____ _____

Review Plurals, Irregular Plurals, and Possessives

Fill in the blanks to complete the chart below.

Singular	Plural	Singular Possessive	Plural Possessive
_____	pianos	piano's	_____
library	_____	_____	libraries'
thief	_____	_____	_____
_____	bicycles	bicycle's	_____
_____	geese	_____	_____
lady	_____	_____	_____
_____	_____	roof's	_____
_____	_____	kangaroo's	kangaroos'
boss	_____	_____	_____
hero	_____	hero's	_____

Rewrite each sentence below, replacing the words in bold with a possessive. Then, underline the plural word or words in the sentence.

1. The **piano teacher of Amira** has given lessons for 40 years.

   _____

2. The **voices of the singers** echoed down the narrow hallways.

   _____

3. The **keys of the pianos** were yellowed with age.

   _____

4. The **orchestra of this city** is well known in many countries.

   _____

Review Plurals, Irregular Plurals, and Possessives

Read the sentences below. Underline the word that correctly completes each sentence.

1. Maine was admitted to the Union at the same time as Missouri, which kept the number of free and slave (states', states) equal.

2. (Thousand's, Thousands) of (islands, islands') lie in the Atlantic Ocean off the coast of Maine.

3. About ninety percent of the land in Maine is covered by (forestes, forests). Most of the (forest's, forests') owners are lumber and paper (companys, companies).

4. (Potatos, Potatoes) are grown in the section of Maine called the New England Upland.

5. (Deers, Deer), black bears, (mouses, mice), raccoons, beavers, bobcats, and (foxes, foxs) are some of the animals that can be found in the woods of Maine.

6. The best time to look for (meese, moose) is dusk or dawn, near the edges of lakes or (ponds, pondes).

7. (Autoes, Autos) are the (mooses', moose's) greatest (enemies, enemys).

On the line, write the plural form of each word below.

1. Eskimo _____   5. loaf _____

2. daisy _____   6. volcano _____

3. goose _____   7. brush _____

4. elf _____   8. pony _____

Lesson 2.7 Compound Words

> A **compound word** is made by combining two shorter words.
>
> air + plane = airplane   book + case = bookcase

Use the pictures to help you fill in the blanks in the problems below.

1. bird + = _____

2. + sauce = _____

3. + print = _____

4. doll + = _____

5. pan + = _____

Read the words in both boxes below. Combine the words to make as many compounds as possible.

Box A (first half of compound)   Box B (second half of compound)

back	food	fire	bath	sea

pack	fall	weed	fly
man	stage	food	flake
robe	tub	yard	storm
place	wood	shell	room

_____

_____

_____

Lesson 2.7 Compound Words

Read the letter below and underline the 15 compound words.

Dear Mom and Dad,

Camp has been so much more fun than I thought it would be.
Every day we do something new. I haven't even been homesick once.

On Friday, we helped the counselors make cupcakes for Anya's
birthday party. Then, we painted flowerpots using homemade paint.
That afternoon, I won the underwater race across the pond.

Last week, we made birdfeeders out of pinecones. I also went
horseback riding twice. There was a thunderstorm one night, so we
stayed inside and made popcorn in the old stone fireplace.
Can't wait to see you on visiting day! I miss you!

Audrey (The Camping Queen)

Now, write the two words that make up each compound from above.

1. _____   6. _____   11. _____

   _____   _____   _____

2. _____   7. _____   12. _____

   _____   _____   _____

3. _____   8. _____   13. _____

   _____   _____   _____

4. _____   9. _____   14. _____

   _____   _____   _____

5. _____   10. _____   15. _____

   _____   _____   _____

Lesson 2.8 Contractions

> • A **contraction** is a short way of writing two words. An apostrophe (')
>   takes the place of the missing letters in a contraction.
>   I am = I'm   they will = they'll   it is = it's   did not = didn't
> • The words will and not form the contraction won't.
> • In a question, the two words that can form a contraction may not
>   be next to one another:
>   Did you not see the sign?   Didn't you see the sign?

Fill in the blanks to complete the problems below.

1. _____ + would = I'd

2. _____ + _____ = they're

3. you + will = _____

4. _____ + _____ = that's

5. _____ + not = won't

6. _____ + _____ = it'll

In each sentence below, there are two words that can be combined to form a contraction. Circle the words and write the contraction on the line.

1. Billy did not miss a word until the end of the
   spelling bee.   _____

2. Antonio could not spell the word silhouette.   _____

3. I am so nervous that my heart is racing.   _____

4. It is lucky that Moriko studied Latin.   _____

5. Has Claire not been to the National Bee before?   _____

Lesson 2.8 Contractions

Read the paragraphs below. Circle the nine contractions. On the lines following the paragraph, write the two words that form each contraction.

The word collage comes from a French word that means to stick. It's a good way to describe the art of collage. The types of materials you use aren't important. You'll just need glue, scissors, and some magazines, newspapers, wrapping paper, or old photos. You shouldn't worry too much about the arrangement of your images. If you like it, you can't go wrong.

Have you ever heard of Eric Carle? He's a popular author and illustrator of children's books. He creates collages to illustrate all of his books. They're usually pictures of animals and insects. Other artists make collages that are abstract. This means that they don't look realistic. If you'd like to make an online collage, visit the National Gallery of Art's Web site.

1. _____   6. _____

   _____   _____

2. _____   7. _____

   _____   _____

3. _____   8. _____

   _____   _____

4. _____   9. _____

   _____   _____

5. _____

   _____

Review Compound Words and Contractions

Look at the pictures below. On the line, write the word from the box that names the picture. Then, circle the two words that form each compound.

| fireworks | basketball | starfish | horseshoe | sailboat | wheelchair |

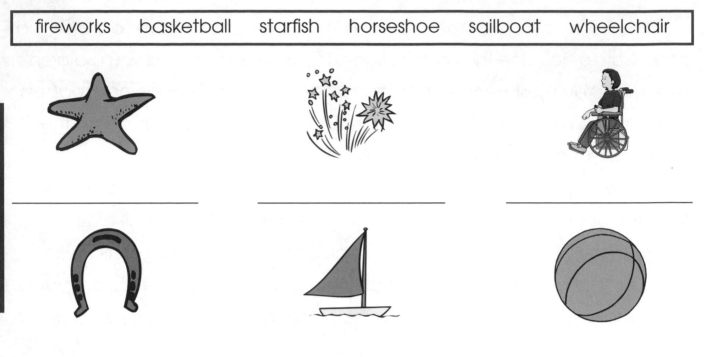

_____   _____   _____

_____   _____   _____

Form a common compound word by drawing a line to match each word in column 1 to a word in column 2. Write the compound word on the line.

1. _____   home   stick

2. _____   bee   box

3. _____   drum   room

4. _____   every   case

5. _____   tool   work

6. _____   scare   crow

7. _____   pillow   where

8. _____   class   hive

Review Compound Words and Contractions

On the first line, write the words that form each contraction below. On the second line, write the letters replaced by the apostrophe.

1. couldn't _____   _____

2. she'll _____   _____

3. I'm _____   _____

4. doesn't _____   _____

5. they're _____   _____

Read the paragraphs below. Circle the 7 contractions and underline the 12 compound words.

James whistled, and his Border collie, Sadie, raced through the barnyard at top speed. She wasn't as fast as she'd been as a pup, but she had grown calmer and more loyal with every passing year. Together, James and Sadie walked toward the farmhouse.

James could smell the blueberry pie his mother was baking. He pictured her in the kitchen, standing before her stained, worn cookbook. In his mind, he could see a bottle of buttermilk sitting on the counter and some cornbread cooling on the stovetop. Everywhere James looked, he was reminded of something he'd miss. He couldn't believe that there would be no more afternoons chasing Sadie through the cornfields or that he wouldn't go to sleep every night listening to the croak of bullfrogs in the pond.

The time had come for James to go away to school. "You'll appreciate it one day," his father had told him. He didn't doubt that his father was right. But that still didn't make it any easier to leave.

Lesson 2.9 Prefixes

Adding a **prefix** to the beginning of a word can change its meaning.
• The prefixes **un-**, **in-**, **im-**, and **dis-** can mean not or opposite of.

unclear = not clear   **dis**like = not like

impolite = not polite   **in**complete = not complete

Read each clue below. Choose the word from the box that matches the clue, and write it on the line.

impossible	invisible	unhurt	unsafe
impatient	disagree	uncommon	disconnect

1. not common _____

2. not hurt _____

3. not possible _____

4. not safe _____

5. not patient _____

6. not agree _____

7. not visible _____

8. not connect _____

Read the sentences below. Choose the word from the box that best completes each sentence, write it on the line, and circle the prefix.

unexpected	impolite	disobeys	unafraid	incorrect

1. My dog rarely _____ when he is given a command.

2. Tony is adventurous and is always _____ of trying new things.

3. If your answer is _____, the computer will make a beeping sound.

4. We received an _____ phone call late last night.

5. I don't mean to be _____, but I don't have time to talk right now.

Lesson 2.9 Prefixes

> • The prefix **re-** can mean again.   **re**fill = fill again
> • The prefix **pre-** means before.   **pre**wash = wash before
> • The prefix **mis-** means wrongly or badly.   **mis**lead = lead badly

Read the recipe below. Find and circle the ten words with prefixes.

Fruit Pizza

Remember, always have an adult present when you are cooking.

- $\frac{1}{2}$ cup butter
- 1 cup sugar
- 1 egg
- $1\frac{1}{4}$ cups all-purpose flour

- $\frac{1}{2}$ teaspoon baking soda
- $\frac{1}{4}$ teaspoon salt
- 8 ounces light cream cheese
- 2 teaspoons vanilla extract

- bananas, pineapple, and prewashed berries and peaches

1. Preheat the oven to 350°. Precut peaches and berries, and set aside.

2. In a large bowl, mix the butter and $\frac{1}{2}$ cup sugar. If it isn't creamy, remix it. Add the egg, flour, baking soda, and salt, and mix until blended. Press the dough into a pizza pan, and bake it for 8 to 10 minutes.

3. In another bowl, beat the cream cheese, $\frac{1}{2}$ cup sugar, and vanilla. Spread this mixture over the cooled crust. Add slices of fruit, and rearrange if needed.

4. Preplan your schedule so you can chill the pizza for three hours before serving. If you misjudged the amount of time you had, just chill it for one hour. The pizza is best when eaten cold. It will not taste good if you reheat it.

5. Try to reuse or recycle any wrappers or containers you can.

Lesson 2.9 Prefixes

> • The prefix **non**- means not or without. **non**washable = not washable
> • The prefix **anti**- means against.   **anti**war = against war

Circle the word with a prefix in each sentence below. On the line, write the definition of the word.

1. Abraham Lincoln was known for his antislavery
   beliefs.   _____

2. Did you ask the librarian if that book is nonfiction? _____

3. Mom squirted antifreeze on the windshield as
   soon as we got in the car.   _____

4. Annabelle's little sister can talk nonstop for hours. _____

5. Mr. Goebelt bought an antitheft device for his
   new car.   _____

6. Sign language is a nonverbal way for people
   to communicate.   _____

Phonics Connection

1. On the lines, write two words from the exercise above in which **s** makes the /z/ sound, as in music.

   _____   _____

2. Find two words from the exercise above in which **s** makes the /s/ sound as in sleep.

   _____   _____

Lesson 2.9 Prefixes

- The prefix **sub**- means under or less than.
  subzero = less than zero
- The prefix **super**- means above, extra, or greater than.
  superhuman = more than human

Read each clue below. On the line, write the word from the box that matches each clue.

subway	supersoft	subzero	subhuman	submarine	superstar

1. a train that travels or makes its way below the ground   _____

2. something that is extra soft   _____

3. something that is less than human or not quite human   _____

4. a vehicle that moves under the water   _____

5. someone very famous; a great star   _____

6. below zero   _____

Read the sentences below. Underline each word that begins with a prefix.

1. The United States is one of the world's superpowers.
2. Some superhighways in large cities have as many as 16 lanes!
3. Taylor giggled as he submerged his toy truck in the bathtub.
4. The muffin recipe calls for superfine sugar.
5. Cat food was on sale at the grocery store, so Mom bought a supersized bag.

Lesson 2.10 Suffixes

Adding a **suffix** to the end of a word can change its meaning.
- The suffix -**ful** means full of. If a base word ends in **y**, change the **y** to **i** before adding -**ful**.   hope**ful** = full of hope
- The suffix -**less** means without.   use**less** = without use

Read the paragraphs below. On each line, write a word with the suffix -**ful** or -**less** to take the place of the words in bold.

The night before the picnic, Sanja felt **without hope** _____.

The weather had been **full of beauty** _____ all week. That

evening, though, a storm that was **full of power** _____ swept

through the area. Sanja felt sure that all her preparations would be **without**

worth _____. It would be **without a point**

_____ to try to have a family picnic in weather like this.

Sanja tossed and turned for hours before she finally fell into a sleep

that was **full of fits** _____. She awoke early after a night that

was nearly **without sleep** _____. A ray of sun drifted across

Sanja's bed. She felt **full of hope** _____ as she peered

outside. A bright blue sky greeted her. Immediately, Sanja felt **full of cheer**

_____. The family picnic was sure to be **full of success**

_____.

Lesson 2.10 Suffixes

- The suffix -**able** means can be or able to be. If a base word ends in **e**, you usually drop the **e** before adding **able**.

  wash**able** = able to be washed

  erase → eras**able** = able to be erased
- The suffix -**en** means made of or to make. If a base word ends in **e**, drop the **e** before adding **en**.

  soft**en** = to make soft   broke → brok**en** = to make broke

For words that have a short vowel sound and end in a consonant, double the consonant before adding **en**.

  hid → hid**den** = to make hid

Add a suffix to each word below. Write the new word on the line. Then, write a sentence using the word you formed.

1. froze + en = _____

   _____

2. value + able = _____

   _____

3. break + able = _____

   _____

4. bit + en = _____

   _____

On the line, write the word that matches each definition below.

1. able to bend _____   3. able to be enjoyed _____

2. to make loose _____   4. to make bright _____

Lesson 2.10 Suffixes

> The suffixes -**ness** and -**ship** both mean state of being or condition of.
> weak**ness** = state of being weak   friend**ship** = state of being friends

Add a suffix to each base word below. Write the new word on the first line. On the second line, write the definition of the word. Then, circle each word in the word search puzzle.

1. bald + ness = _____   _____

2. happy + ness = _____   _____

3. citizen + ship = _____   _____

4. kind + ness = _____   _____

5. friend + ship = _____   _____

6. owner + ship = _____   _____

7. smooth + ness = _____   _____

b	c	i	t	i	z	e	n	s	h	i	p	b	k	u	y
a	h	t	n	n	w	o	w	n	e	r	s	h	i	p	t
l	x	w	q	j	a	b	l	e	y	m	b	b	n	n	s
d	d	f	r	i	e	n	d	s	h	i	p	e	d	e	p
n	h	f	m	r	u	d	h	q	i	n	v	x	n	c	a
e	l	o	b	r	w	u	v	r	v	a	a	j	e	p	m
s	h	y	q	n	f	h	a	p	p	i	n	e	s	s	n
s	m	o	o	t	h	n	e	s	s	g	t	z	s	i	o

Lesson 2.10 Suffixes

> • The suffix -**ish** means like, about, or somewhat.
>   baby**ish** = like a baby
> • The suffix -**ment** means action or process.
>   treat**ment** = the action of treating

Read the sentences below. Add **ish** or **ment** to each word in parentheses to correctly complete the sentence. Remember, you may need to change the spelling of the base word before you add the suffix.

1. I'll meet you at the restaurant around _____. (six)

2. I saw an _____ for it in the newspaper. (advertise)

3. Have you eaten _____ food before? (Spain)

4. My whole family is in _____ that a rice dish called paella is the tastiest. (agree)

5. The restaurant is in a _____-brown building. (red)

6. Some nights, they even have live _____. (entertain)

Read each clue below. On the line, write a word that ends in **ish** or **ment** and matches each clue.

1. the process of arranging   _____

2. the action of governing   _____

3. like a girl   _____

4. around fifty   _____

5. the action of being amazed   _____

Review Prefixes and Suffixes

Use the table to help you remember the meanings of the prefixes you have learned.

un-, **in-**, **im-**, **dis**- = not or opposite of	**mis**- = wrongly or badly
re- = again	**non**- = not or without
pre- = before	**anti**- = against
super- = above, extra, or greater than	**sub**- = under or less than

Read the clues below. Write the word from the box that matches each clue.

antipollution   impure   nonfiction   subzero   indirect   unlucky

1. not lucky _____

2. below zero _____

3. not pure _____

4. against pollution _____

5. not direct _____

6. not fiction _____

Circle the nine words that have prefixes in the paragraphs below.

Today, my aunt and cousins are moving here from Mexico. They'll live in our apartment until they find a place of their own. Dad was worried because his phone calls home went unanswered for several weeks. Suddenly, he received an unexpected letter that told him his sister would arrive in three days! My dad reread that letter four times to be sure he didn't misread a word.

First, he sent my brother and me to the supermarket. He preordered some groceries and prepaid for them over the phone. Rafael and I raced to the steps of the subway. For the next three days, we worked nonstop. They're due to arrive at any minute, so I'd better get downstairs!

Review Prefixes and Suffixes

Use the table to help you remember the meanings of the suffixes you learned. Remember, the spellings of some base words change when a suffix is added.

-ful = full of	**-ness, -ship** = state of being
-less = without	**-ish** = like, about, or somewhat
-able = can be or able to be	**-ment** = action or process
-en = made of or to make	

Add a suffix to each word below. Write the new word on the line. Then, write a sentence using the word you formed.

1. happy + ness = _____

_____

2. hid + en = _____

_____

3. agree + ment = _____

_____

Read the paragraph below. On each line, write a word with a suffix to take the place of the words in bold.

The library is my favorite place in the world because its supply of

books seems **without end** _____. It always **makes bright**

_____ my day to visit the kids' section. I've found that almost

any question in the world is **able to be answered** _____ when

I'm at the library. I'm **full of doubt** _____ that I could think of

a more **able to be enjoyed** _____ place to spend the day.

Lesson 2.11 Syllables

Words can be divided into parts called **syllables**. Each syllable has one vowel sound. The number of vowel sounds in a word is equal to the number of syllables.

glass = 1 vowel sound = 1 syllable
in·sect = 2 vowel sounds = 2 syllables
fac·tor·y = 3 vowel sounds = 3 syllables
un·u·su·al = 4 vowel sounds = 4 syllables

Look at each picture below. Choose the word from the box that names the picture, and write it on the first line. On the second line, write the number of vowel sounds you hear when you say the word aloud.

alligator   hammer   banana   watermelon   cricket   bike

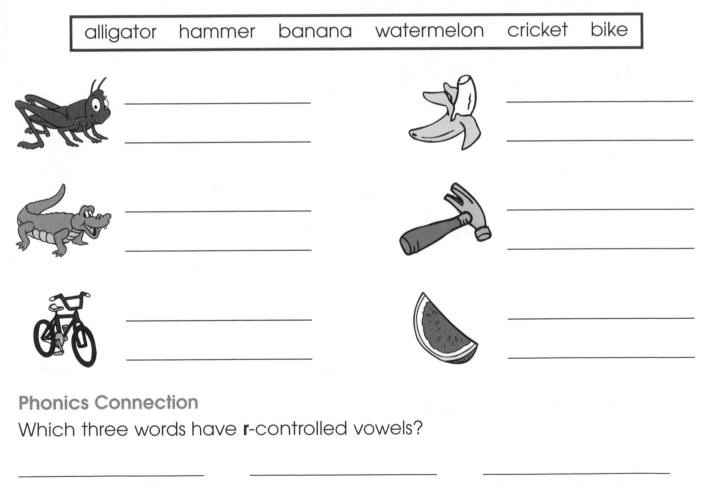

Phonics Connection

Which three words have **r**-controlled vowels?

_____   _____   _____

Lesson 2.11 Syllables

- Compound words can be divided into syllables between the two parts of the compound.
     gold·fish   hand·shake
- A word that has two consonants between two vowels (VCCV) can be divided between the consonants.
     cir·cus   al·ways
- A word that has a prefix or suffix can be divided between the prefix or suffix and the base word.
     un·wind   help·ful

Read the words in bold below. Draw slashes to divide each word into syllables. Then, circle the word beside it that has the same number of syllables.

1. **football**	subject	icicle	multiply
2. **dislike**	difficult	pillowcase	cheerful
3. **thunder**	bell	subway	kangaroo
4. **mislead**	plant	reuse	supermarket
5. **doorknob**	cactus	honestly	wonderful
6. **nonstop**	tablespoon	plate	kindness

Underline each two-syllable word in the sentences below. Then, draw a slash to divide each underlined word into syllables.

1. Did Bella take the subway to the zoo on Friday?
2. I must have misread the directions, but I can recheck them before we leave.
3. Danny and Maria took a basket of homemade pretzels to Mrs. Pasalis.
4. It was hard to see through the darkness without a flashlight.

Lesson 2.11 Syllables

When you see a word that has the vowel-consonant-vowel pattern (VCV), listen carefully to the first vowel sound you hear.
- If it has a long sound, the word is usually divided after the first vowel.
    e·ven   m**o·me**nt
- If it has a short sound, the word is usually divided after the consonant.
    t**rav·e**l   **lem·o**n

Read the words below. Underline the VCV pattern in each word. On the line, write long if the first vowel sound is long, and short if it is short.

1. second _____   **5.** comet _____

2. pilot _____   **6.** photo _____

3. major _____   **7.** metal _____

4. sliver _____   **8.** over _____

Read each clue below. On the line, write the word from the box that matches the clue. Draw a slash through the word to divide it into syllables.

female	minus	pedal	lemon	rhino

1. an African animal that has a large horn _____

2. the opposite of male _____

3. a sour yellow fruit _____

4. the part of a bicycle on which you rest your feet _____

5. the math symbol used in subtraction _____

Lesson 2.11 Syllables

Read the paragraphs below. Draw slashes through each word in bold to divide it into syllables.

What do **penguins**, whales, **dolphins**, and seals have in **common**? They are all good **swimmers**. In fact, they are such good swimmers that **scientists** are studying their fins and **flippers**. Scientists are trying to **figure** out why these marine animals can move so quickly and easily **underwater without** a lot of **effort**. Ships, and other water **vehicles**, are moved by **propellers**. A boat that could stop immediately or that could make its way through tight **spaces** would be **safer** and more **useful**.

A penguin's flippers don't just spin **around** like a propeller does. They can move in all sorts of **directions**. A boat of the **future** might have as many as 50 flippers that could **allow** it to move in many directions too. Scientists are also studying the fins of **animals** like dolphins. **Unlike** a propeller, fins are **flexible**. Scientist have been **trying** fins and flippers made from different kinds of materials in their **experiments**. They have to **rebuild** their projects over and over before they get them right. Can you **recall** **anything** else made by humans that **imitates something** from nature?

Phonics Connection

1. Which word in paragraph 1 has the silent consonant pair **sc**?

_____

2. Which word in paragraph 1 has the long **o** sound spelled **oa**?

_____

Review Syllables

On the line, write the word that names the picture. Then, circle the word beside it that has the same number of syllables.

1. _____ wild   forever   spaceship

2. _____ subject   banana   joyful

3. _____ secret   climb   terrible

4. _____ monkey   scream   unclear

Read the words below, and fill in the blanks in the chart.

	Vowel Sounds Heard	Number of Syllables
1. invention		
2. comet		
3. tornado		
4. chimp		
5. cowboy		
6. motorcycle		
7. girlish		
8. meatless		
9. activity		
10. skip		

Review Syllables

Read the words in the box. Write each word below the correct heading. Then, draw slashes to divide the words into syllables.

> mistreat   grin   playpen   north   vacation   chimney
> press   popular   flame   marvelous   adventure   pupil

1 syllable	2 syllables	3 syllables
_____	_____	_____
_____	_____	_____
_____	_____	_____
_____	_____	_____

Read the sentences below. Draw slashes through each word in bold to divide it into syllables.

1. Paintings by **famous** artists can be worth thousands or **millions** of **dollars**.
2. Some **dishonest** people try to **copy** the paintings and sell them as **originals**.
3. **Researchers** have found a way to tell the real paintings from the fakes.
4. They start with a **digital** image of the **painting**.
5. A **computer** uses a math **technique** to break this image into smaller pieces.
6. The researcher can **compare** the painting to **pictures** of the original.
7. If the brush strokes look the same, then the painting is **likely** to be real.
8. The brush strokes of fake paintings look different from each **other**, and they **also** look different from the rest of an artist's work.
9. It won't be long **before** crooked **artists** are out of a job!

Lesson 3.1 Synonyms

Synonyms are words that have the same or almost the same meanings.

pick, choose   injure, hurt   scream, shout

Draw a line to match each word in column 1 to its synonym in column 2.

1. odor	courageous
2. start	smell
3. brave	gift
4. present	begin
5. repair	mend

Read the sentences below. On the line, write a synonym from the box for each word in bold.

worried   tugged   seem   enjoy   several   children   entire   huge   yelling

On Saturday, I had my first baby-sitting job. I **like** _____

spending time with **kids** _____, but I had no idea what I was

getting myself into.

Jasmine and Dominic have an **enormous** _____

amount of energy. They **pulled** _____ each other's hair,

raced through the house **screaming** _____, and knocked

over a **whole** _____ gallon of chocolate milk.

I was **concerned** _____ that it would **appear**

_____ that I didn't have everything under control. Luckily, I

brought along a **few** _____ of my little brother's books. In no

time, the twins were being as good as gold.

Lesson 3.1 Synonyms

Circle the word from the pair in parentheses that correctly completes each sentence below.

1. Another word for donate is (take, give).

2. To trade is the same as to (win, exchange).

3. A person who is happy is a person who is (worried, glad).

4. The words sour and (sweet, tart) mean the same thing.

5. A synonym for sloppy is (messy, sleepy).

6. Another word for wreck is (build, destroy).

Read each set of words below. On the line, write the letter of the word that is a synonym for the word in bold.

1. _____ **tasty**   **a.** yummy   **b.** rotten   **c.** spicy

2. _____ **beautiful**   **a.** ugly   **b.** pretty   **c.** strange

3. _____ **yank**   **a.** move   **b.** slide   **c.** pull

4. _____ **thin**   **a.** heavy   **b.** slender   **c.** strong

5. _____ **freedom**   **a.** liberty   **b.** belief   **c.** taste

6. _____ **throw**   **a.** catch   **b.** keep   **c.** toss

7. _____ **usual**   **a.** weird   **b.** common   **c.** old

Phonics Connection

1. Which three words in exercise 2 begin with a three-letter blend?

   _____   _____   _____

2. On the lines, list the two words in exercise 2 that have the hard **c** sound.

   _____   _____

Lesson 3.2 Antonyms

An **antonym** is a word that means the opposite of another word.

dirty, clean   front, back   frozen, melted

Circle the two words that are antonyms in each riddle below.

1. **Q:** How does Mother Earth fish?

   A: With North and South Poles.

2. **Q:** Which is faster—hot or cold?

   A: Hot, because you can catch a cold.

3. **Q:** Give me food and I will live. Give me water and I will die. What am I?

   A: A fire.

4. **Q:** I have holes in my top and my bottom, but I still hold water. What am I?

   A: A sponge.

5. **Q:** What's black and white and red all over?

   A: An embarrassed skunk.

6. **Q:** I am a place where yesterday follows today. What am I?

   A: A dictionary.

7. **Q:** What goes up and never comes down?

   A: Your age.

8. **Q:** Which is heavier, and which is lighter—a ton of gold or a ton of feathers?

   A: Neither. They weigh exactly the same—one ton.

Lesson 3.2 Antonyms

Read each sentence that follows. Circle the word below it that is an antonym for the word in bold.

1. The Native American Arapaho (ə rap' ə hō') live in **western** states like Colorado, Kansas, and Wyoming.

   warmer   eastern   larger

2. Like **many** other Native American tribes, they have their own government, laws, and police.

   few   always   most

3. In the **past**, the Arapaho people lived in tents called tipis that were made of buffalo skin.

   before   future   created

4. Men and **women** wore their hair in long braids.

   men   babies   farmers

5. **Before** the invention of cars, the Arapaho used horses to travel and to carry their things from one place to another.

   usually   maybe   after

6. Originally, the Arapaho were farmers, but once they had horses, they **followed** buffalo herds.

   borrowed   led   used

Phonics Connection

1. Which word in bold ends with the long **e** sound? _____

2. Which word in bold has an ending blend? _____

Review Synonyms and Antonyms

Read the clues below. Find the word in the box that matches each clue, and write it in the numbered space in the crossword puzzle.

forget	cure	enter	early	insect	pass
	choose	following	asleep	locate	

Across
1. a synonym for bug
5. a synonym for after
6. an antonym for awake
8. a synonym for select

Down
2. an antonym for late
3. a synonym for find
4. an antonym for exit
5. an antonym for remember
7. an antonym for fail
8. a synonym for heal

Review Synonyms and Antonyms

Read the paragraphs below. If the word in bold is followed by an **A**, find an antonym from the box and write it on the line. If it is followed by an **S**, find a synonym and write it on the line.

observe	started	ordinary	journey	smallest	same
Earth	last	incredible	evenings	perfect	something

Something very **special** (A) _____ happens during the

first (A) _____ week of October every year. Thousands of

people gather in Albuquerque, New Mexico, to **watch** (S)

_____ the sky fill with hundreds of brightly-colored balloons.

The Albuquerque International Balloon Fiesta lasts for nine days. It is the

largest (A) _____ gathering of balloonists around the **world**

(S) _____. About 750 hot air balloons and their pilots make

the **trip** (S) _____. As many as 100,000 people may come to

watch the **amazing** (S) _____ sight.

The festival **began** (S) _____ in 1972. Only 13 balloons

came that year, but the fiesta, or celebration, has grown larger every year.

One of the reasons the fiesta is held in Albuquerque is that the weather is

ideal (S) _____ on October **mornings** (A)

_____. It is usually clear and cool. There is **nothing** (A)

_____ quite like seeing the crisp, blue sky filled with balloons

in every color of the rainbow.

Lesson 3.3 Shades of Meaning

In Lesson 3.1, you learned that synonyms are words that have the same or almost the same meanings. When the meanings are not exactly the same, you have to think carefully about which word fits best in a sentence.

For example, the words divide and split mean almost the same thing, but they have different shades of meaning. In the sentence below, split makes more sense than divide.

Mrs. Murray had to split up the students who were talking.

Mrs. Murray had to divide up the students who were talking.

Read the sentences below. Underline the word from the pair in parentheses that best completes each sentence.

1. Whenever I see Grandma, she pinches my cheeks and (gives, donates) me a kiss on the forehead.

2. I knew Uncle Albert would be able to (mend, fix) the broken radio.

3. (Grab, Take) the leash before the dog escapes!

4. Andrew (made, built) the cake himself.

5. Can you give us (a model, an example) of what you mean?

6. If you (hear, listen) closely, you can tell the difference between the songs of the two birds.

7. Maya did the (right, correct) thing, even though it was hard for her to do.

8. The antique doll is (value, worth) nearly $100.

9. Kenji would like some more milk and a second (piece, part) of pie.

Lesson 3.3 Shades of Meaning

Read the sentences below. Choose the word from the box that best completes each sentence and write it on the first line. Then, find another word from the box that means almost the same thing and write a sentence using it.

coin	pushed	sharp	injury	wound	stop
quit	late	shoved	pointed	overdue	money

1. My pencil is not nearly _____ enough to finish this drawing.

   _____

2. Mr. Abu-Jaber _____ the baby carriage down the street.

   _____

3. I found the most valuable _____ in my collection online.

   _____

4. If you don't hurry, we'll be _____ for the movie.

   _____

5. Sophie trained the puppy to _____ and sit before they cross a road.

   _____

6. The quarterback's old _____ has bothered him for years.

   _____

Phonics Connection

Which two words in the box above have the same vowel diphthong?

_____   _____

Lesson 3.4 Levels of Specificity

Some words give the reader more information than others.
- A general word, like animal, gives the reader basic information. A more specific word, like dog, gives the reader an added detail. The word sheepdog, is more specific than both animal and dog.
- Here is another example: color → purple → lavender

Purple tells the reader what color, and lavender tells the shade of purple.

Read the sets of words below. Number the words in order from least to most specific, with **1** being least specific and **3** being most specific.

Ex.: penny __3__   currency __1__   coin __2__

1. snake _____   reptile _____   black adder _____

2. furious _____   mad _____   feeling _____

3. daisy _____   flower _____   plant _____

4. size _____   large _____   enormous _____

5. canoe _____   vehicle _____   boat _____

6. fruit _____   orange _____   food _____

Match each word in column 1 with a more specific word in column 2.

1. cry   yank

2. mammal   wail

3. quiet   wrench

4. pull   monkey

5. tool   silent

Lesson 3.4 Levels of Specificity

Read each clue and the set of words that follow it. Choose the word that is most specific and circle it.

1. I am crunchy and orange, and I have a leafy green top. Rabbits love me.

   food   carrot   vegetable

2. I am white with black spots. You'll often find me at fire stations.

   dog   animal   Dalmatian

3. I am a sweet drink. I am made from fruit and water.

   juice   liquid   beverage

4. I am large, blue, and filled with waves and undersea animals. I can be found along the East Coast of the United States.

   water   ocean   Atlantic

5. You can play me with a black and white ball. Remember not to use your hands!

   sport   soccer   ball game

6. I was first popular among African Americans in the South. If you listen to me, you'll probably hear a saxophone, a trumpet, and a piano.

   jazz   sound   music

7. People often sleep inside me when they go camping. It doesn't take long to set me up.

   shelter   tent   structure

8. I am a part of your body. You'll find me between your ankle and knee.

   leg   limb   shin

Review Shades of Meaning and Levels of Specificity

One word in each sentence below does not quite fit. Find the word and cross it out. On the line, write the word from the box that would better fit the sentence.

| pack | eat | wild | meaning | weak | have | cut |

1. Molly and I filled our buckets with untamed raspberries. _____

2. Saw the paper into four equal pieces. _____

3. It took Nibori about an hour to fill his suitcase. _____

4. Christopher's muscles felt feeble after he spent a week in bed with the flu. _____

5. I understand most of the French words in the story, but what is the purpose of the word jamais? _____

6. Lexi and Bryan both own dentist appointments on Thursday. _____

7. Remember, you need to consume your vegetables if you want to have dessert. _____

Read the sentences below. Underline the word from the pair in parentheses that best completes the sentence.

1. Be careful, your shoelaces are (loose, untied).

2. What did the snake's skin (touch, feel) like?

3. Try to (record, write) as much of the conversation as you can.

4. Today was perfect. I wouldn't (revise, change) a single thing.

5. The (summit, peak) of the gingerbread house was decorated with yellow icing.

Review Shades of Meaning and Levels of Specificity

On the line, rewrite each set of words below in order from general to specific.

1. color   indigo   blue

   _____

2. candy   licorice   sweets

   _____

3. cloth   towel   dishrag

   _____

4. France   country   place

   _____

Look at the pictures, and read the sentences below. Use a word from the box to fill in each blank.

drums   clock   diamond   hawk   watch

1. The word _____ is more specific than bird.

2. A jewel is a type of mineral, and a _____ is a type of jewel.

3. A _____ is a specific type of _____, which is a specific type of timepiece.

4. Bongos are a more specific kind of instrument than _____.

Lesson 3.5 Homophones

Homophones are words that sound the same but have different spellings and meanings.

Please shoo the fly away from the brownies.

The right shoe feels a little too tight.

Circle the word that correctly names each picture. Use a dictionary if you need help.

horse   hoarse   scent   cent   dear   deer

bawl   ball   pair   pear   serial   cereal

wring   ring   plane   plain   tale   tail

Phonics Connection

Find the homophone pair from above in which both words have the /aw/ sound, as in raw.

_____   _____

Lesson 3.5 Homophones

Read the paragraphs below. Underline the word from the pair in parentheses that correctly completes each sentence.

My (aunt, ant) and uncle have just returned from a wild and eventful trip. I told them that (there, their) journey was exciting enough to be (maid, made) into a movie. It all started about a (week, weak) ago. Aunt Miki and Uncle Ted decided to (sale, sail) to the South Carolina (See, Sea) Islands from a port near their home in Massachusetts. The first (phew, few) legs of the (cruise, crews) went off without a hitch. They (heard, herd) that there (mite, might) be (sum, some) bad weather near North Carolina, but they weren't (two, too) worried. They must have (missed, mist) the reports that warned them to avoid the exact area they were headed for.

The waves were (high, hi), and the heavy (reign, rain) made it hard for them to see. Their (clothes, close) were soaking wet, but they stayed above deck anyway. With each gust of wind, Aunt Miki could (here, hear) the sails (creak, creek) and groan. She was worried the boat (wood, would) start to (leek, leak), but she didn't say a word to Uncle Ted.

It felt as though they had battled the storm for (eight, ate) hours, but it actually lasted closer to three (ours, hours). When the rain and wind finally stopped battering their boat, Uncle Ted and Aunt Miki each breathed a sigh of relief. The (sun, son) peeked out from behind the stormy gray clouds, and they (new, knew) that they were safe. I think it'll (be, bee) a while before my aunt and uncle are ready for another adventure.

Lesson 3.6 Multiple-Meaning Words

A **multiple-meaning word**, or **homograph**, is a word that has more than one meaning. Use the context of a sentence to determine which meaning the author intends.

Did you hear the phone ring?   Molly made a ring for her mom.
The law firm has eight members.   The peach is firm but ripe.

Read each sentence and the definitions that follow. Circle the letter of the definition that matches the word in bold.

1. Did the Herreras' dog **bark** when you rang the doorbell?

    a. the hard covering of a tree trunk   **b.** the sound a dog makes

2. The rec center is building a new baseball **diamond** at the park.

    a. a valuable gemstone   **b.** a baseball infield

3. **Coat** the pan with cooking spray.

    a. cover   **b.** a jacket

4. The old **trunk** had sat in my grandparents' attic for nearly 60 years.

    a. a container for storing things   **b.** an elephant's snout

5. Carefully **seal** the envelope before you mail the letter.

    a. a sea mammal   **b.** to tightly close

6. The **fair** comes to town every year during Labor Day weekend.

    a. a festival or carnival   **b.** just; equal

7. Every Saturday night, my grandparents play **bridge** with their neighbors.

    a. a structure built over water   **b.** a card game

Lesson 3.6 Multiple-Meaning Words

Read each sentence below. On the line, write a sentence using another meaning of the word in bold. If you need help, use a dictionary.

1. I watched the water **pool** on the floor near the leaky pipe.

   _____

2. Every bed in Grandpa's cabin has a thick **down** comforter made from goose feathers.

   _____

3. The cat's **pupils** got larger and larger in the dim light.

   _____

4. A **school** of bright yellow fish swam lazily through the coral reef.

   _____

5. What **kind** of fruit would you like to have with your lunch?

   _____

6. The **hatch** of the submarine opened, and the captain poked out his head.

   _____

7. Please buy a **pound** of apples, a dozen eggs, and a gallon of milk.

   _____

Phonics Connection

Which two words in bold contain a diphthong? Circle the diphthong in

each word. _____   _____

Lesson 3.7 Word Play

> • **Onomatopoeia** (on' ə mat' ə pē' ə) refers to words like crash, oink, squish, and boom that are similar to the sounds they describe.
> • A **palindrome** is a word or sentence that reads the same forward and backward. Peep, mom, and Madam, I'm Adam, are examples of palindromes.

Circle each example of onomatopoeia you find in the sentences below.

1. Ding-dong went the doorbell. I was so surprised, I bonked my head on the cupboard door.

2. "Hmmm," I said. "Who could that be?"

3. Cameron clomped into the house wearing his heavy winter boots.

4. My parakeet cheeped and twittered in her cage when she heard our voices.

5. Cameron rustled around in his bag. "You're going to love this new computer game I got for my birthday," he murmured.

6. He inserted the disc into the drive, and the living room filled with the clanging and buzzing of the machines on the screen.

7. Cameron grinned as a whooshing sound poured out of the speakers.

Make a check mark beside the palindrome in each pair below.

1. _____ Did Hannah say as Hannah did?   _____ Was it a pet I saw?

2. _____ deed   _____ keep

3. _____ stop   _____ toot

4. _____ Too bad I hid a yam.   _____ No lemons, no melon.

5. _____ Now sir, a game is won.   _____ Ma handed Edna ham.

Lesson 3.7 Word Play

A **portmanteau** (pôrt' man tō') word is a word that contains parts of two other words. It is different from a compound word because it contains only parts of the words, not the entire words.

flutter + hurry = flurry   blow + spurt = blurt

Use the words in the box to solve the problems below.

| clap   scrawl   wipe   guestimate   shimmer   humongous   chuckle |

1. _____ + sweep = swipe

2. guess + estimate = _____

3. scribble + sprawl = _____

4. _____ + snort = chortle

5. gleam + _____ = glimmer

6. _____ + crash = clash

7. huge + monstrous = _____

Complete each sentence below with a portmanteau word from the box.

| brunch   moped   smog   Internet |

1. My entire family is coming over to eat _____ on Sunday morning.

2. Diego found some helpful Web sites on the _____.

3. Luke wears a helmet when he rides his _____.

4. During the summer, _____ in big cities can be thick.

Review Homophones, Multiple-Meaning Words, and Word Play

Circle the homophones that correctly complete the paragraph below.

Many scientists are worried about something called global warming. During Earth's history, (they're, there) have (been, bin) a number of changes in the (weather, whether) and climate. Some cases, like Ice Ages or droughts, are extreme. In the last 100 years, it (seams, seems) that the average temperature on (hour, our) planet has increased (by, buy) about .6° Celsius.

Even though this may (knot, not) seem like a lot, it can have a (grate, great) effect on animal and plant life. In places where scientists used to (fined, find) certain wildlife, it has disappeared. They (know, no) that even a small change in temperature can change an animal's food supply. It can also affect whether (hole, whole) species of plants survive. The temperatures today are changing faster than ever. What will this mean (four, for) all living creatures?

Read the definitions and the sentences below. Make a check mark beside the sentence that uses the word in bold the way it is defined.

1. **date** noun the month, day, and year

    _____ What is today's date?   _____ Ali and John went on a date.

2. **bill** noun a notice of payment due

    _____ The duck's bill is brown.   _____ The waiter gave Mom the bill.

3. **batter** noun a dough-like mixture

    _____ Mix the batter in the bowl.   _____ The batter stepped up to the plate.

4. **present** noun a gift

    _____ Your present is in the box.   _____ Mr. Rao will present the award.

Review Homophones, Multiple-Meaning Words, and Word Play

Read each set of onomatopoeic words below. Choose the word from the box that names the animal or thing that would be most likely to make those sounds.

horse	thunderstorm	bird	cereal	rain	human

1. _____ cheep, chirp, tweet

2. _____ snort, whinny, clip-clop

3. _____ hurray, oops, giggle, ah-choo

4. _____ snap, crackle, crunch

5. _____ drip, drop, pitter-patter

6. _____ crash, bang, boom

Read the words and phrases in the box. Underline each palindrome you find.

cool	Nurses run.	dream	Roy, am I a mayor?	level
stool	Top spot.	racecar	spots	Don't nod.
gag	Never odd, and never even.	noon	sleep
toot	Rise to vote, sir.	Step on few pets.	radar

On the line, write the letter of the portmanteau word that matches each pair of words in column 1.

1. _____ slap + lather   **a.** scrunch

2. _____ squeeze + crunch   **b.** flop

3. _____ twist + whirl   **c.** twirl

4. _____ flap + drop   **d.** slather

NAME _____

Lesson 3.8 Figures of Speech

A **simile** is a comparison of two unlike things using the words like or as.
Halley's new jacket fits her like a glove.
A **metaphor** is a comparison of two unlike things without using like or as.
My legs were rubber as I stepped up to the microphone.

Circle the simile in each sentence below.

1. The plump, ripe cherries were as sweet as honey.

2. After weeks without rain, the backyard was dry as a bone.

3. The icy snow crunched like popcorn beneath our boots.

4. The clouds were like puffs of cotton candy scattered through the sky.

5. Dressed in his snowsuit, the toddler waddled like a penguin across the yard.

Read the metaphors below. On the lines, tell which two things are being compared.

1. The thumping of Rachel's heart was a steady drumbeat in her chest.

_____   _____

2. The tornado was a monster that destroyed everything in its path.

_____   _____

3. The baby's teeth were tiny white pearls that sparkled when she smiled.

_____   _____

4. The grass was a velvety carpet beneath our bare feet.

_____   _____

5. The sirens were wild shrieks that tore into the night.

_____   _____

Lesson 3.8 Figures of Speech

Read each sentence below. If it contains a metaphor, circle **M**. If it contains a simile, circle **S**.

1. **M S** Lightning lit the sky like fireworks on the Fourth of July.

2. **M S** The train was a speeding bullet that shot past the station.

3. **M S** The songbirds were a symphony outside Elizabeth's window.

4. **M S** The night after the storm, icicles dangled like earrings from every tree branch.

5. **M S** The little boy was a fierce warrior as he attacked his dinner.

6. **M S** Before the skaters arrived, the ice in the rink was as smooth as glass.

Read the paragraphs below. Underline the four similes. Circle the two metaphors.

Our first night at Greystone Park was incredible. For dinner we cooked juicy burgers over the campfire. The fresh corn on the cob was as yellow as sunshine, and the cherry tomatoes burst in our mouths like tiny water balloons. After dinner, we sat quietly in the darkness. Wisps of smoke from the fire danced into the sky like twirling and leaping ballerinas. At home, I'd probably be watching TV or playing on the computer, but I don't miss either of those things here. The darkness is a thick warm blanket that makes me feel cozy and safe with my family.

It's so much louder here than it is outside our apartment. Somehow, though, the night sounds of the woods are a soothing lullaby. Sleep washes over me like a wave, and I finally stop fighting to stay awake.

Lesson 3.9 Idioms

An **idiom** is a group of words that mean something other than what they appear to mean. For example, The new employee bent over backward to please his boss means that the person made a great effort or tried very hard.

Read each idiom in column 1. On the line, write the letter of the definition in column 2 that best matches each idiom.

1. _____ got the ball rolling   **a.** stay with it; don't give up

2. _____ lost his temper   **b.** to talk or chat

3. _____ cold feet   **c.** to feel nervous

4. _____ call it a day   **d.** something simple; very easy

5. _____ shoot the breeze   **e.** to have a talent for growing plants

6. _____ make ends meet   **f.** go to bed

7. _____ green thumb   **g.** know or understand how things work

8. _____ a piece of cake   **h.** to make a certain amount of money cover expenses

9. _____ know the ropes   **i.** became angry

10. _____ hit the hay   **j.** to quit or be finished

11. _____ hang on   **k.** got things started

Phonics Connection

Which three words above have the long **a** sound spelled **ay**?

_____ _____ _____

Lesson 3.9 Idioms

Read the paragraphs below. Underline the seven idioms you find.

On Saturday morning, Blanca and her friends rode their bikes to Mill Creek Park. They were joining their neighbors and some local businesses to help clean up the park. Mr. Wu, the organizer of the cleanup, spoke to the crowd that had gathered at the gates of the park.

"I'm so pleased to see you all," he began. "This park belongs to all of us. If no one cared about our public spaces, we'd all be in the same boat. If we stick together, we can make amazing things happen!"

The crowd cheered, grabbed their recycling bags, and put on rubber gloves. Blanca, Louie, and Sara headed for the park trail. As they picked up trash, it dawned on Blanca that the environment wasn't just something she learned about at school or on TV. Blanca decided that caring about the environment was something worth sticking out her neck for.

A couple of hours later, the group gathered again. They snacked on bagels and hot cider as Mr. Wu beamed at the crowd. He looks like he has something up his sleeve, Blanca thought to herself.

"As you know, we have people from several different businesses here today. I asked them for donations for GreenSpace Kentucky. I thought there was a slim chance we'd raise much money this way, but I was wrong. They've offered to donate a total of $5,000 dollars to our cause!"

The owner of a local bakery grinned and shook her head. "Mr. Wu drives a hard bargain," she said. "How could we say no?"

Review Figures of Speech and Idioms

Find the figure of speech in each sentence below. If it is a simile, underline it. If it is a metaphor, circle it.

1. The warm chicken noodle soup was as comforting as a hug.
2. The tree branches were like fingers that reached toward the old house.
3. The terrible secret was a heavy load that Cassie carried with her.
4. The morning sun was a cheery invitation for Jack to get up.
5. The flock of blackbirds burst into the sky like a handful of confetti.

Choose four things that were used in a comparison in the exercise above. On the lines below, write four sentences of your own using new comparisons.

For example, the sun was compared to an invitation. A new comparison might be The sun was a fat yellow balloon hanging in the blue October sky.

1. _____
2. _____
3. _____
4. _____

Phonics Connection

Use the words in the first exercise to answer the questions below.

1. On the lines, write three words that begin or end with a digraph.

   _____ _____ _____

2. Which word contains a vowel diphthong? Circle the diphthong.

   _____

Spectrum Word Study and Phonics
Grade 4
142

Review: Lessons 8–9
Vocabulary

REVIEW: CHAPTER 3 LESSONS 8-9

Review Figures of Speech and Idioms

Read each definition below. On the line, write the idiom from the box that matches the definition.

down in the dumps	on cloud nine	felt like a million dollars
dead to the world	all in the same boat	neck and neck
set someone straight	stole the spotlight	plain as the nose on his/her face

1. fast asleep _____

2. very close together in a race _____

3. to be in the same situation as others _____

4. to correct someone _____

5. to be extremely happy _____

6. something obvious or hard to miss _____

7. felt special, important, or terrific _____

8. felt depressed or blue _____

9. got all the attention _____

Choose four idioms from the box in the first exercise. Write four sentences of your own using the idioms you chose.

1. _____

2. _____

3. _____

4. _____

Lesson 4.1 Alphabetical Order

Words are arranged in **alphabetical order** (or **ABC order**) in dictionaries, encyclopedias, indexes, and libraries.

When two words start with the same letter, use the second letter to decide the order. If the first two letters of the words are the same, use the next, and so on.

afraid, **b**lend, **f**erry   p**a**rent, p**i**g, p**o**lar   le**o**pard, le**t**ter, le**v**el

Read each pair of words below. On the line, write the word that comes between them in ABC order.

1. minute _____ mixed   mine   mist   mink

2. nibble _____ nickname   nice   nowhere   notion

3. picture _____ place   pizza   plaid   pester

4. splash _____ starfish   statue   stencil   squat

5. expire _____ factor   exhaust   fabulous   enjoy

6. disobey _____ dispose   disk   dispatch   dispute

7. filling _____ flute   flounder   fiddle   field

Read each set of words below. On the lines, number the words in ABC order.

1. _____ jelly   _____ jeep   _____ jazz

2. _____ lens   _____ length   _____ lentil

3. _____ mislead   _____ niece   _____ miss

4. _____ rear   _____ quarrel   _____ polish

5. _____ weigh   _____ weirdo   _____ weekly

6. _____ cocoa   _____ coconut   _____ coax

Lesson 4.1 Alphabetical Order

Read the paragraphs below. On the numbered lines that follow, write the words in bold in ABC order.

Hint: It may help to organize the words on a scrap sheet of paper first.

Zydeco is an exciting, fast-paced **form** of **folk** music. It has its roots in southwest Louisiana, among the French-speaking **Creole** and **Cajun** people. An **accordion**, a **washboard**, a saxophone, drums, and a guitar are typical instruments in a zydeco **band**. The **African** music that was a base for early rhythm and blues also played a role in early zydeco music. The **first** recordings were made by Amédé Ardoin in 1928.

Even though it **became** somewhat **popular** in the 1950s, zydeco never really became a big hit the way rock music or **jazz** did. Still, **anyone** who hears the fast, **bouncy** beat has a hard time keeping their **toes** from **tapping** or their **fingers** from **snapping**. It's the kind of music that makes people want to move.

1. _____   8. _____   15. _____

2. _____   9. _____   16. _____

3. _____   10. _____   17. _____

4. _____   11. _____   18. _____

5. _____   12. _____   19. _____

6. _____   13. _____   20. _____

7. _____   14. _____

Phonics Connection

List the six words in bold that have an **r**-controlled vowel.

_____   _____   _____

_____   _____   _____

Lesson 4.2 Guide Words

Guide words are found at the top of a dictionary page. They tell you the first and last word on that page. If the word you are searching for comes between the guide words in ABC order, it will be on that page of the dictionary.

For example, the word falcon would be on the page that has the guide words failure and false because it comes between them in alphabetical order.

Read each set of guide words below. On the line, write the letter of the word that would appear on a dictionary page with them.

		a.	b.	c.
1.	_____ foal — folder	flutter	foil	flyer
2.	_____ rumble — Russian	rusty	rye	runway
3.	_____ jester — jockey	jellyfish	jewel	jerk
4.	_____ gravel — greedy	gross	ground	grease
5.	_____ boost — borrow	booth	botany	bottle
6.	_____ thumb — tickle	through	ticket	thread

Look up each of the following words in a dictionary. On the line, write the guide words from the page on which you found the word.

1. jaguar _____   _____

2. weather _____   _____

3. daisy _____   _____

4. blueberry _____   _____

5. steal _____   _____

Lesson 4.2 Guide Words

Read each word below. Use the pair of guide words to decide on which dictionary page you would find the word. Write the page number on the line.

hail — hammer page 97	hammock — hanger page 98	silk — sink page 220	skill — sled page 222

1. _____ haircut

2. _____ handsome

3. _____ silo

4. _____ halfway

5. _____ hamburger

6. _____ slavery

7. _____ silly

8. _____ handkerchief

9. _____ skylark

10. _____ halo

11. _____ simple

12. _____ hamster

13. _____ skim

14. _____ handwriting

Read each pair of guide words and the set of words listed below them. Underline each word in the set that could be found on the same page as the pair of guide words.

trade — transform

traffic

treat

tragedy

trap

transmit

trampoline

sandpaper — Saturday

sandwich

salmon

sank

sari

sand

sauce

Lesson 4.3 Entry Words

When you look up a word in a dictionary, you are looking up an **entry word**. An entry word is usually printed in bold. Most entry words are base words. For example, you would look up jump, not jumping and baby, not babies.

entry word   pronunciation & syllables   part of speech   meaning

sailor (sā′ lər) noun a person who sails; often the member of a ship's crew

Read each word below. On the line beside it, write the entry word.

1. sunnier _____

2. laughing _____

3. sandwiches _____

4. whispered _____

5. busiest _____

6. buzzes _____

7. splitting _____

8. mangoes _____

Use the dictionary entry below to answer the questions.

second (sek′ ənd) 1. noun a unit of time; 1/60 of a minute
2. adj. coming after the first; number two

1. How many syllables does second have? _____

2. Which syllable is stressed in second? _____

3. Which part of speech is second in this sentence?
There are only 16 seconds left until halftime. _____

Lesson 4.3 Entry Words

Read the paragraphs below. Write the entry word beside each word in bold.

Sports _____ seem to be in LeBron James's blood. As a

high school junior, he decided to concentrate on basketball. **Judging**

_____ from his many **successes** _____ on the

court, this seems to have been a good choice.

LeBron James stands 6 feet 8 inches tall and **weighs**

_____ 240 pounds. He has been an NBA player for the

Cleveland Cavaliers since 2003. LeBron has been **compared**

_____ to basketball greats like Michael Jordan. While he

was still in high school, he **drew** _____ national attention. As

a high school junior, he wanted to take part in the NBA draft. The **rules**

_____ state that an athlete must finish high school first, and

LeBron was **told** _____ he had to wait.

During his first year playing **professionally**_____, LeBron

won _____ Rookie of the Year. In 2005, he became the

youngest _____ player to score 4,000 career points. LeBron

has had quite a career, and he keeps getting better!

Review Alphabetical Order, Guide Words, and Entry Words

Juliana is having a movie marathon party. She has made a list of movies she might rent. Fill in the blanks with titles from the box. Make sure that the list stays in ABC order. Hint: Ignore the word the at the beginnings of titles.

The Rookie	The Incredibles	The Secret of Roan Inish
Robots	The Wizard of Oz	Because of Winn-Dixie
The Princess Bride	Spy Kids	Atlantis: The Last Empire

Anastasia

_____

_____

The Road to Eldorado

_____

_____

Bedknobs and Broomsticks

Ice Age

_____

The Secret Garden

_____

Shrek 2

_____

Madagascar

_____

Toy Story 2

_____

The Princess Diaries

Rewrite the following words in ABC order.

1. dreamy, driftwood, dress, drench _____

2. hook, honest, hood, honey_____

3. spider, spoil, spindle, spicy _____

4. brew, broccoli, breed, bridle_____

5. mole, mold, moist, model _____

Review Alphabetical Order, Guide Words, and Entry Words

Each heading below is a set of guide words from a dictionary page. Write the words from the box under the correct headings.

motor   moon   motel   mud   moor   mouse   moral   motto   mown

monument — more

_____

_____

_____

moss — mound

_____

_____

_____

mourn — muffin

_____

_____

_____

Use the dictionary entries below to answer the questions that follow.

meadow (med′ ō) noun a grassy field

maybe (mā′ bē) adv. perhaps; possibly

match (mach) pl. matches **1.** noun a small piece of wood used for starting fires
2. verb to put two similar things together

1. Put the entry words above in ABC order.

_____ _____ _____

2. What is the plural form of match?   _____

3. Which of the words above would you find on a dictionary page with the guide words mattress and measles?   _____

4. Which syllable is stressed in maybe?   _____

On the line, write the entry word you would look for in a dictionary.

1. cities _____   4. bunches _____

2. clapping _____   5. mosquitoes _____

3. peacocks _____   6. yelled _____

Lesson 4.4 Pronunciation Key and Respellings

Next to each entry word in a dictionary, there is a **respelling** of the word. The respelling includes special letters and symbols that show how the word should be pronounced.

A **pronunciation key** is a guide to using the letters and symbols found in respellings. A pronunciation key is usually found on every other page in a dictionary.

Use the pronunciation key below to answer the questions in this lesson.

PRONUNCIATION KEY

/a/	= **at**, t**a**p	/u/	= **u**p, c**u**t	/ə/	= a (**a**round, **a**bout)
/ā/	= **a**pe, s**ay**	/ū/	= **u**se, c**u**te		e (bett**e**r, tak**e**n)
/ä/	= f**a**r, h**ea**rt	/ü/	= r**u**le, c**oo**l		i (rabb**i**t, penc**i**l)
/â/	= c**a**re, h**ai**r	/u̇/	= p**u**ll, b**oo**k		o (doct**o**r, lem**o**n)
		/û/	= t**u**rn, v**e**rb		u (**u**pon, circ**u**s)
/e/	= **e**nd, g**e**t				
/ē/	= **e**ven, m**e**	/ch/	= **ch**in, tea**ch**		
/ê/	= p**ie**rce, f**ea**r				
		/ng/	= si**ng**, ha**ng**		
/i/	= **i**t, f**i**t				
/ī/	= **i**ce, t**ie**	/sh/	= **sh**op, ru**sh**		
/o/	= h**o**t, f**a**ther	/th/	= **th**in, bo**th**		
/ō/	= **o**ld, s**o**	/<u>th</u>/	= **th**is, smoo**th**		
/ô/	= s**o**ng, b**ou**ght				
/ȯ/	= f**o**rk, c**o**rn	/hw/	= **wh**ite, **wh**y		
/oi/	= **oi**l, b**oy**				
/ou/	= **ou**t, h**ou**se	/zh/	= trea**s**ure, bei**ge**		

On the line, write the letter of the word that matches each respelling.

1. _____ /nōm/

2. _____ /bub' əl/

3. _____ /rō' dē ō'/

4. _____ /strāt/

5. _____ /brü net'/

6. _____ /rīt/

7. _____ /tôl/

8. _____ /guv' ərn mənt/

9. _____ /trezh' ər/

10. _____ /strēm/

a. straight
b. tall
c. right
d. bubble
e. government

f. gnome
g. stream
h. brunette
i. treasure
j. rodeo

Lesson 4.4 Pronunciation Key and Respellings

Read each clue below and the respelling that follows. Say the respelling out loud to yourself. On the line, rewrite the word that matches the clue.

1. a traveling show that has animals and clowns /sûr′ kəs/ _____

2. a large gray mammal that has a long trunk /el′ ə fənt/ _____

3. a person who can keep several objects moving in the air at once /jug′ lər/ _____

4. a high wire that a performer crosses /tīt′ rōp/ _____

5. a wild cat that has a large, shaggy mane /lī′ ən/ _____

6. a person who dresses up in funny clothes, does tricks, and makes people laugh /kloun/ _____

7. a person who performs stunts /ak′ rə bat′/ _____

Read each letter or set of letters below. Use the pronunciation key to figure out its sound. Underline the word or words beside it that contain the same sound.

1. /ā/   sailboat   male   ramp   action
2. /j/   gentle   growl   justice   gift
3. /âr/   part   Clare   wear   heart
4. /oi/   oyster   toast   cold   voyage
5. /ū/   raccoon   custom   amuse   cute

Phonics Connection

List one word in exercise 2 in which **s** makes the /s/ sound and one in which it makes the /z/ sound.

_____   _____

Lesson 4.4 Pronunciation Key and Respellings

Read the paragraphs below. On the line, rewrite each respelling.

Sojourner Truth was the name that Isabella Van Wagener gave to

herself. Isabella was born a /slāv/ _____. Slaves /ô′ fən/

_____ took the last name of their master. /Wuns/

_____ she was free, Isabella gave herself a new name. It

may have /bin/ _____ a way for her to shed the past and

give herself a fresh start in the /wûrld/ _____.

Sojourner was granted her freedom in 1827. She spoke out /ə genst′/

_____ slavery /ev′ rē hwâr′/ _____ she went.

/Lärj/ _____ groups of people gathered to hear her

speeches. With a /frend/ _____, she wrote her biography,

called The Narrative of Sojourner Truth.

In the 1850s, Sojourner /bē cām′/ _____ involved with

women's rights. She began speaking about them /wen/

_____ she gave speeches /ə bout′/ _____

slavery. It was unusual at that time for women to talk about their rights, but

Sojourner wasn't /ə frād′/ _____ of what anyone else /thôt/

_____. She /stúd/ _____ her ground and had

faith in what she believed to be just and /rīt/ _____.

NAME _____

Lesson 4.4 Pronunciation Key and Respellings

Read each respelling and the set of words that follows it. Circle the word the respelling stands for.

1. /jen′ tl/   genuine   jiggle   gentle
2. /tō′ təm/   total   totem   tortoise
3. /wā/   weigh   wait   wall
4. /ē nuf′/   easy   tough   enough
5. /fyū′ chər/   fuse   future   further

Read the sentences below. Underline the words that the respellings in the box stand for.

/sum/	/i maj′ in/	/ri mōt′/	/līk/	/īs/	/di zēz′/
/ā′ zhə/	/clām/	/livd/	/krē′ chər/	/mil′ yən/

1. Imagine a shaggy animal the size of an elephant that weighs about seven tons and has tusks 15 feet long.

2. It sounds like a made-up creature, but at one time, wooly mammoths lived in Europe, Africa, Asia, and North America.

3. Experts believe that the mammoth lived between 1.6 million years and 10,000 years ago.

4. No one is sure if mammoths died out because of an Ice Age, disease, or overhunting.

5. Some people claim to have seen mammoths in remote parts of Siberia during the last 100 years. Nothing has ever been proven, though.

Lesson 4.5 Accent Marks

An **accent mark** (') tells which syllable of a word is stressed. The stressed syllable is said with more force.
- In /lō' shun/, the first syllable is stressed. Try saying the word lotion with the stress on the second syllable. Can you hear the difference?
- Remember, the schwa does not appear in stressed syllables.

Read each respelling below aloud to yourself. Listen to which syllable is stressed and underline it. If you are not sure, trying stressing different syllables when you say the word.

1. /sōl jər/
2. /hôk ē/
3. /rü bē/
4. /ə round/
5. /ri fyūz/

6. /pə līs/
7. / mə skē tō/
8. /roi əl/
9. /skwē kē/
10. /pə tā tō/

Read each pair of words below. Say the words to yourself and circle the letter of the word that has the accent in the correct place.

1. **a.** /sik' nis/   **b.** /sik nis'/
2. **a.** /ə gō'/   **b.** /ə' gō/
3. **a.** /prâr ē'/   **b.** /prâr' ē/
4. **a.** /shuf' əl/   **b.** /shuf əl'/
5. **a.** /dout fəl'/   **b.** /dout' fəl/
6. **a.** /pə' līt/   **b.** /pə līt'/
7. **a.** /hûr' mit/   **b.** /hûr mit'/
8. **a.** /ə' fend/   **b.** /ə fend'/

Lesson 4.5 Accent Marks

Read the paragraphs below. The words in bold are followed by their respellings. Add an accent (') to each to show which syllable is stressed.

Emmanuel strolled **along** (ə lông) the sidewalk in front of his school, watching for his friend Matt. **Several** (sev ər əl) days each week, they met after school and walked **together** (tə geth ər) to the rec center to play chess. Emmanuel preferred having **plenty** (plen tē) of time to think about each move, but Matt liked it **better** (bet ər) when they used the clock.

Suddenly, Matt came **running** (run ing) out of the school's front door. Matt **explained** (ik splānd) that he had just **spoken** (spō kən) to Mr. Sanchez, the **principal** (prin sə pəl). He had agreed to join Emmanuel and Matt on **Thursdays** (thûrz dāz) to teach them new chess strategies. With a little help, the boys felt sure their game would improve in no time.

Some multiple-meaning words are spelled the same but pronounced differently. The word record can be pronounced /rek' ərd/ or /ri kôrd'/. The meaning is different depending on the accents and pronunciation.

Underline the respelling that correctly completes each sentence below.

1. What time will Mr. Klein (/pri zent'/, /prez' ent/ his speech?
2. Kyle was stationed in the (/di zûrt'/, /dez' ərt/) for two years.
3. Who will (/kən dukt'/, /kôn' dukt/) the orchestra this year?
4. "I (/ob' jikt/, /əb jekt'/)," said the judge, pounding his gavel.
5. Santhe's favorite (/sub' jikt/, /səb jekt'/) is English, but she likes science, too.

Review Respellings and Accent Marks

Use the pronunciation key on the inside back cover of this book to answer the questions that follow.

1. Which symbol stands for the vowel sound in lake? _____

2. What are the pronunciation key words for the
    /th/ sound?   _____

3. Which symbol stands for the vowel sound you
    hear in clip?   _____

4. According to the pronunciation key, what are
    two pairs of letters that can make the /zh/ sound? _____

5. Which symbol stands for the ending sound
    in photo?   _____

6. Which letters can make the /ə/ sound?   _____

Read the sentences below. Circle the words that the respellings in the box stand for.

/sed/	/bôgz/	/fēldz/	/nā′ tiv/	/en joi′/
/grōn/	/ev′ rē/	/kun′ trē/	/flōt/	

1. For many people, cranberries are part of Thanksgiving dinner every year.

2. Some people also enjoy eating these tart berries in muffins or cakes.

3. It is said that the native people introduced the cranberry to English
    settlers in the early 1620s.

4. Today, cranberries are grown in bogs in northern parts of the country.

5. The fields are flooded when it is time to harvest.

6. When the bushes are shaken, the ripe berries float to the top of the water.

Review Respellings and Accent Marks

Look at the pictures below. Choose the respelling from the box that matches each picture, and write it on the line. Add an accent mark (') to each respelling to show which syllable is stressed.

/flou ûr/	/win dō/	/tī gər/	/ba lā/	/trezh ər/
/sûr kəl/	/zē brə/	/bə lün/	/jak it/	

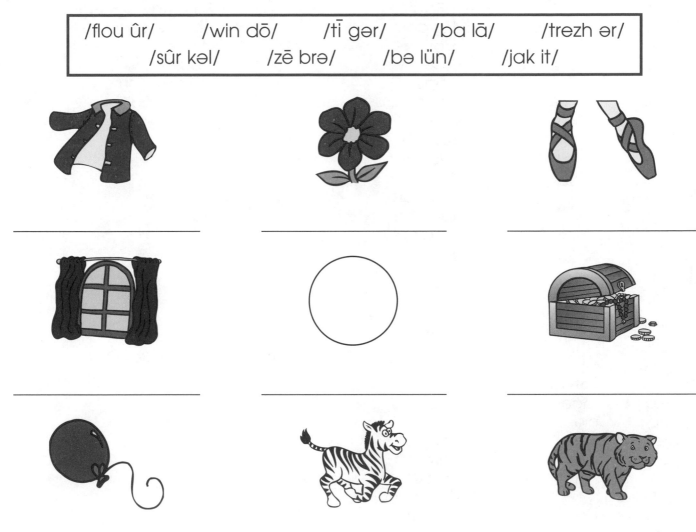

Read each pair of respellings below. Say the words to yourself and underline the word that has the accent in the correct place.

1. /ban dij'/   /ban' dij/

2. /nûr' sə rē/   /nûr sə rē'/

3. /ə round'/   /ə' round/

4. /sad l'/   /sad' l/

5. /chêr ful'/   /chêr' ful/

6. /hu rā'/   /hu' rā/

Answer Key

page 6

(f)eather
fox

(h)ouse
hippo

(l)ion
latch

(k)ite
key

1. beach
2. tub
3. nine
4. cave
5. sock

page 7

fla(g)
wig

gras(s)
hiss

be(ll)
grill

an(t)
get

ma(sk)
ask

6

si(x)
mix

1. star
2. trip
3. list
4. fort

page 8

Hard c	Soft c
caring	race
camp	cider
code	ice
cute	rice

flag; hard **g**
giraffe; soft **g**
cage; soft **g**
garden; hard **g**

page 9
1. hard **g**
2. soft **g**
3. hard **c**
4. soft **c**
5. soft **g**
6. soft **c**
7. hard **g**

8. hard **c**

1. gorilla
2. crab
3. Egypt
4. grape
5. bridge
6. celery
7. tiger
8. mice

page 10
1. fancy
2. ago
3. candle
4. bridge
5. camera
6. gem

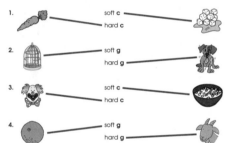

page 11
Hard c	Soft c
coin	piece
American	center
called	
can	

Hard g	Soft g
games	ages
tag	large
again	
tagged	
goal	
good	
great	

page 12
1. always, busy
2. usually
3. is, sure
4. Saturday, days, best
5. cheese, salad, music, stereo
6. stack, news
7. measure, times
8. these, traditions

page 13
1. singing
2. yours
3. measure
4. sugar
5. those
6. silly

1. s; z
2. z
3. s
4. z
5. s
6. s; s; zh

page 14
1. b, n, l
2. c, s, c, m
3. t, W, d, t, t
4. l, d
5. p, c
6. T, p

1. hard
2. soft
3. hard
4. soft
5. hard
6. hard
7. soft
8. soft

Answer Key

page 15

flag   bridge
jug   energy
fog   danger

carrot   mice
clam   cent
climb   place

1. bus, bus
2. visitors
3. most, famous, buses
4. /s/ seated, passengers
   /z/ passengers
5. most
6. /zh/ treasured
   /z/ use, busses, preserve

page 16
1. scale
2. spinach
3. sneeze
4. stegosaurus

1. Stella and Spencer put on sweaters and wrapped scarves around their necks.
2. They spent every fall evening swinging from the old oak tree.
3. Stella scanned the sky for constellations. Stella and Spencer were keeping score to see who could spot more stars.
4. Spencer liked the way the air smelled like smoke from backyard bonfires.
5. When it was time to go back inside, Stella and Spencer snuggled into their beds. They knew that snow was coming, and fall would soon be over.

page 17
1. slow
2. plum
3. flossing
4. clothing
5. glass
6. slippers
7. black

1. bleach — classic
2. flame — glitter
3. plaid — blouse
4. cliff — plump
5. glance — flatten

page 18
1. Georgia, the graceful grasshopper, likes to nap on a patch of green grass on the ground.
2. The prince and princess are prisoners who are given only pretzels and prunes to eat.
3. Drew, the dreadful dragon, is a drummer for a band called the Dizzy Dragonflies.
4. Every day Brittany brushes and braids her hair on the bridge by the brook.
5. Crabs, crayfish, and other critters creep and crawl across the ocean floor.

1. drill
2. brag
3. freed
4. bridge

Possible Answers:
<u>grow</u>
<u>prowl</u>
<u>dress</u>
<u>break</u>
<u>crumb</u>

page 19
twig; two; quarterback
question mark; twirl; quotes

1. twins
2. twelve; twenty
3. Queen; quails
4. quilts

page 20
1. split
2. squeaky
3. Spread
4. squirrels
5. screws
6. sprain
7. square dancing

page 21
1. squeeze
2. thought
3. spread
4. splinter
5. think
6. scribble

1. a type of seafood (shrimp, shrub)
2. thin string used for sewing (threat, thread)
3. a sweet, red, summer fruit (strawberry, streamer)
4. another word for *creek* or *brook* (scrape, stream)
5. to tear into tiny pieces (squawk, shred)
6. another word for *road* (streak, street)
7. what you use to swallow (throat, three)
8. the opposite of crooked (straight, split)

page 22
ft; lift   st; crust
lt; salt   nk; trunk

1. belt
2. drank
3. blast
4. tart
5. find

page 23

1. pact — exact
2. kept — scalp
3. pitchfork — except
4. hurt — bark
5. gulp — skirt

rd; rd; rk; ld; sp; rt; rk

page 24
sc; gl; st
bl; qu; cr

1. switch
2. plumber
3. great
4. twist
5. blonde
6. snarl
7. quart
8. statue
9. trailer
10. sketch
11. prepare
12. cluster

page 25
1. spl
2. shr; squ
3. str
4. shr
5. thr
6. scr

Answer Key

1. something that can be proven true; not an opinion ___ fact
2. what a beach is covered with ___ sand
3. a place people can store their money ___ bank
4. a person whose job is to keep swimmers safe ___ lifeguard
5. a large vegetable that is a deep purple color ___ eggplant

page 26

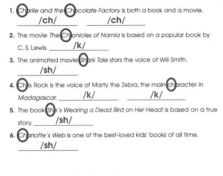

1. *Charlie and the Chocolate Factory* is both a book and a movie.
   /ch/   /ch/
2. The movie *The Chronicles of Narnia* is based on a popular book by C. S. Lewis. ___ /k/
3. The animated movie *Shark Tale* stars the voice of Will Smith.
   /sh/
4. *Chris Rock* is the voice of Marty the Zebra, the main character in *Madagascar*. ___ /k/ ___ /k/
5. The book *She's Wearing a Dead Bird on Her Head!* is based on a true story. ___ /sh/
6. *Charlotte's Web* is one of the best-loved kids' books of all time.
   /sh/

page 27
1. thought
2. flea
3. them
4. whisper
5. hospital

1. Phoebe the spy used a phony passport to travel from Philadelphia to the Philippines.
2. I think that thirty-three people are invited for Thanksgiving dinner.
3. When you have finished whisking four eggs, please whip some cream while I set the table.

Possible answers:
phone
thorn
wheel

page 28
ph; sh; ch
th; ch; sh

1. wash
2. pinch
3. month
4. graph
5. south
6. beach

page 29

1. When writing a paper, each **paragraph** should contain sentences that are about the same topic.
2. The babies ___ **splash** water on their parents at the kiddie pool.
3. A huge ___ **branch** from the maple tree snapped during the ice storm.
4. The **phonograph** was the most common way of playing music for more than 100 years.
5. For dinner, we ate grilled ___ **fish** , mashed potatoes, and green beans.
6. Angelina came in ___ **fourth** at the National Spelling Bee.

1. rich; such
2. mash; rush; blush
3. growth; sixth
4. autograph; telegraph
5. bunch; which; trench
6. push; ash
7. tooth; math

page 30
swing; strong
stick; rack
laugh; tough
clock; thick

rough; learning; laugh;
Looking; back; spending;
storytelling; listening

page 31

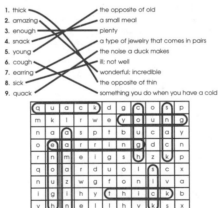

1. thick — the opposite of thin
2. amazing — wonderful; incredible
3. enough — plenty
4. snack — a small meal
5. young — the opposite of old
6. cough — something you do when you have a cold
7. earring — a type of jewelry that comes in pairs
8. sick — ill; not well
9. quack — the noise a duck makes

page 32

1. dumb	grab	crumb	tub
2. kneel	kiss	karate	never
3. writing	rules	windy	whisper
4. science	scream	scent	crush
5. tomb	sob	zoom	crab

Read the sentences below. Choose the word from the box that best completes each sentence. Write it on the line. Then, cross out the silent letter.

| climb | knew | limb | wrong |

1. As soon as Leah heard the meows, she ~~k~~new her cat was stuck in a tree.
2. Daisy thought she could get down alone, but she was ~~w~~rong
3. "If you help me get the ladder, I can clim~~b~~ up there and rescue Miss Daisy," said Leah's dad.
4. "Why does she always get stuck on the highest lim~~b~~ ?" he asked.

page 33
1. thumb
2. knit
3. scientist
4. writer
5. lamb
6. knapsack
7. scissors
8. wrist
9. kneel
10. wring

1. crum~~b~~ glum
2. ~~k~~new stew
3. ~~w~~reath beneath
4. ~~k~~nuckle chuckle
5. tom~~b~~ groom
6. ~~k~~nead freed
7. s~~c~~ent rent
8. lim~~b~~ trim

page 34
1. budge; ledge; badge
2. watch; pitch; scratch
3. gnarled; gnawed; design
4. Tonight's; flight; might; weigh
5. patchwork; matches; fetch
6. headlights; straight; thigh

page 35
dg; gh; tch
gn; dg; gh
tch; gh; dg

1. pledge

Answer Key

2. crutch
3. fight
4. gnat
5. scratch

page 36
brush; shout
phone; photo
ring; strong
chef; Chicago

1. ch
2. sh
3. sh
4. gh; ck
5. Wh; ck; th

page 37
thumb; scissors
wreath; match

1. ju~~d~~ge
2. assi~~g~~n
3. ~~K~~nocked
4. ~~W~~rinkled
5. eyesi~~gh~~t
6. crum~~b~~

page 38
shot; vest; punch; wax;
fast; finch; jog; chance;
trip; mug; will

1. Answers will vary.
2. Answers will vary.

page 39
1. wig
2. leg
3. sick
4. truck
5. quack
6. stop

7. fist
8. tent

1. pick; sniff
2. thank; sand
3. shot; frog
4. flash; gasp
5. stiff; cling
6. bunch;stuck
7. swam; plant
8. click; grin

page 40

1. scrap + e = __scrape__
2. twin + e = __twine__
3. plum + e = __plume__
4. rod + e = __rode__
5. past + e = __paste__

fume
drape
waste
code
spine

1. doe
2. true
3. lake
4. spine
5. whale

page 41

Long a	Long i
made	nice
Kate	ride
ate	price
date	grime
	wipe
	shine
	pile

Long o	Long u
vote	June
Joe	blue
shone	Luke
hose	huge
chrome	

page 42
1. space
2. junk

3. knock
4. wide
5. those
6. limp
7. wrap

snake; Answers will vary.
flag; Answers will vary.
lion; Answers will vary.
nose; Answers will vary.
kite; Answers will vary.
drum; Answers will vary.

page 43
short **a**; short **u**; short **a**;
short **a**; short **o**; short **i**

1. long **a**; short **e**; long **o**.
2. long **u**; long **o**; long **o**;
   short **o**; short **i**; short **e**;
   long **i**
3. short **u**; short **i**
4. short **e**; short **u**

long **a**; short **a**; short **i**

page 44
1. pass
2. catch
3. branch
4. also
5. rash

birthday	sleigh	train
say	weigh	bait
spray	neigh	afraid
tray	eight	snail

page 45
1. veil
2. stray
3. they
4. paid

Answer Key

5. hay
6. plate
7. freight
8. play
9. crate; snail
10. prey

page 46

ee; streak   ie; alley

1. I am a southern state. My capital is Nashville.   Tenness**ee**
2. I am a game played in an ice rink on skates. You need a stick and a puck to play.   hock**ey**
3. The son of a brother or sister is a *nephew*. I am the daughter of a brother or sister.   ni**e**ce
4. I am a small bird that is often kept as a household pet.   parak**ee**t
5. I am a story that your mind makes up while you sleep.   dr**ea**m

ea; seaweed   ey; beast

Romanos' Grocery	World Mart and Co.	Lincoln's
apples	**birdseed**	jeans for Olivia
bananas	vitamins	jacket for Marco
parsley	**three** rolls of paper towels	socks
tomatoes		**handkerchiefs**
green onions	dog **treats**	soccer **jerseys**
honey	birthday card	
peanut butter	tinfoil	
dinner rolls	sugar**free** gum	
sliced turkey	**beach** towels	
four **pieces** of catfish	printer paper	
milk	**bleach**	
sour **cream**	can opener	
	tweezers	

page 47

1. breeze
2. sweet
3. wheat
4. bleed
5. shield

page 48

1. wild; child
2. remind; rewind
3. might; fright
4. find; rind
5. night; light
6. wild; mild
1. sight
2. shine
3. unkind

4. wild

page 49

1. behind
2. midnight
3. wind
4. high
5. mild
6. blind
7. wild
8. unwind

tonight	mild	behind
starlight	wilder	blindly
uptight	stepchild	kindest
flight		winding
delight		grind

page 50

old	ow
oa	ow
oa	ow

1. mold
2. stroke
3. host
4. shown
5. throat
6. coach

1. On a gray, wet day, Mr. Watkins and his wife took a __str**oll**__ by the river. (stroll, school)
2. They stopped in surprise when they heard a __gr**oa**n__ coming from the water. (goose, groan)
3. A man was __fl**oa**ting__ on a piece of driftwood in the chilly water! (couch, floating)
4. Mr. Watkins ran back to his car for a piece of rope to __t**ow**__ the man to safety. (block, tow)
5. "I __alm**os**t__ gave up thinking someone would spot me," said the man, huddled in Mrs. Watkins' jacket. (almost, chop)
6. "What were you doing in the water on such a __c**old**__ day?" asked Mrs. Watkins. (pool, cold)
7. "I took my __r**ow**boat__ out to test the new oars I just bought," he replied. (rowboat, frog)
8. "A tree limb snapped and cracked my boat," he added. He __sh**ow**ed__ the Watkins where the branch had injured his leg. (showed, hound)
9. "I guess today was my lucky day," he __t**old**__ his rescuers. (pond, told)

page 51

page 52

throat; note   tree; degree
veil; mail   train; contain

1. bleach; between
2. spray; weigh
3. blind; midnight
4. mold; foam

page 53

long **a**; long **i**; long **o**; long **e**; long **o**; long **e**; long **e**; long **a**; long **e**; long **a**; long **o**; long **e**; long **e**; long **i**

page 54

book	broom
hood	zoo
overlook	classroom

screw   fruit

One **afternoon** the Lyle family entered a contest and won a four-day **cruise**. They packed their **suitcases** and **flew** to Florida. When they arrived, there were **groups** of bright **balloons** all around the ship's deck. Jenna and Will couldn't wait to put on their bathing **suits** and hop in the **pool**.
Just past **noon** the ship's whistle **blew** and the Lyles were on their way. They had a light lunch of **soup** sandwiches **fruit** and fresh **juice** Will stretched out on his towel with a __good book__ while Jenna went swimming. Mrs. Lyle grinned. "It **looks** like four days won't be long enough for any of us!"

cashew	suit
threw	bruise

1. I am eaten like a vegetable, but I am actually a type of fungus. stoop   mush**room**   juice
2. I am a group of people who work together on a boat or a plane. cr**ew**   school   caboose
3. I am a black-and-blue mark on your skin when you get hurt. goose   review   br**uise**
4. I am a type of soup that usually contains chunks of meat and vegetables. st**ew**   scoop   group
5. I am a type of formal clothing. I include a jacket and pants or a skirt. scoot   s**uit**   hook
6. I am an animal that carries my baby in a pouch. I live in Australia. cartoon   kanga**roo**   raccoon
7. I am a kind of bird. zoom   group   g**oose**
8. I am a homograph for, or a word that sounds the same as, *threw*. thr**ough**   tool   though
9. I am the material that covers a caterpillar before it turns into a butterfly. balloon   soup   coc**oon**
10. I am a type of soap used for washing hair. sham**poo**   drool   youth

Answer Key

page 55

page 56
1. sauce
2. claw
3. salt
4. hall
5. caught
6. lawn
7. malt
8. hawk

page 57
1. au
2. aw
3. au
4. all
5. au
6. au

1. southpaw
2. baseball
3. Roll; lawn
4. launch
5. autograph
6. law
7. assault

page 58
1. avoid; destroy
2. appoint; royal
3. spoil; voyage

1. Oink is the sound a pig makes.
2. Clothes can be made out of a soft type of material called corduroy
3. Oysters are a type of shellfish that are often served at seafood restaurants.
4. A cowboy is a person who cares for cattle on a ranch.
5. Something that is rotten is spoiled
6. A shiny silver material used for covering food is called foil

4. moist; Floyd; joint
5. toilet; employ

6. pinpoint; foil; annoy

page 59
1. voice
2. noise
3. voyage
4. asteroid
5. avoid
6. loyal
7. destroyed
8. choice
9. rejoicing
10. joy

page 60
1. Eva's grandma travels south for the winter.
2. The clown made balloon animals at the birthday party.
3. Who spilled grape juice all over the couch?
4. We need to find a crown to complete Jake's costume.
5. Oscar climbed to the top of the lighthouse and looked for ships.
6. Stratus and cumulus are different types of clouds.

page 61

You'll find milk in the refrigerator of almost every house in America. People drink it, pour it on their cereal, and cook with it. Do you know where milk comes from? How does it get from a cow to your kitchen table?

Dairy farms are located all around the country, but many are found in the Midwest. Farmers feed cows a mixture of hay, barley, corn, cottonseed, grasses, and grocery store leftovers. A single cow eats as much as 80 pounds a day! Cows drink a large amount of water too—about 40 gallons daily.

A mother cow produces around eight gallons of milk a day. In the past, people milked by hand. The farmer would crouch on the ground or sit on a stool beside the cow. He or she would squeeze out milk into pails from the cow's udders. Today, cows go to a milking parlor where they are hooked up to a powerful machine. It cools the milk and pumps it into big storage containers. This is faster and easier than milking by hand. Using the machines allows farmers to have more cows.

The milk is picked up every day by a special truck. The metal tanks store the milk and keep it cool as it travels to a processing plant. Now the milk is heated to kill any bacteria. It is put into bottles and cartons and shipped to grocery stores all across the nation. Where would we be without dairy farmers? There is no doubt that they are a very important part of the food industry.

page 62

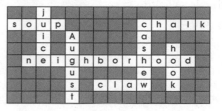

page 63
1. The firefighters decided they needed a dog at the firehouse.
2. Captain Fox said they should go to the pound to find a dog who needed a good home.
3. It didn't take long for them to make their choice.
4. The captain was proud to say that Dixie chose Squad 615.
5. He knew she would be a good friend and a loyal dog.

1. oo
2. all
3. oy
4. aw
5. au
6. ow

page 64
1. An atlas is a book that contains maps.
2. You can find a map of China on page 42.
3. On which page did you find information about the Grand Canyon?
4. We are going to drive across the country in a rental car.
5. Grandpa Louis keeps a travel log of all the places he has been.
6. Use a pencil to jot down these directions.
7. Let's plan to stop at the cactus garden in New Mexico.

1. tunnel
2. tractor
3. final
4. alone
5. cruel
6. gallop

page 65

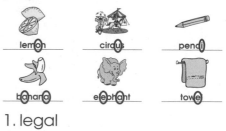

lemon   circus   pencil

banana   elephant   towel

1. legal
2. canoe

Answer Key

3. children
4. classical
5. even
6. possum
7. often

page 66

1. When Max turned seven he had his birthday party at the zoo.
2. Max's favorite part of the zoo is the Serpent House.
3. He knows all the snakes by their common names.
4. Greenbrook Zoo keeps about 500 snakes at the Serpent House.
5. Max's friends agree that snakes are the most interesting reptiles.
6. The zookeeper feeds the snakes small mammals like mice and rats.
7. Snakes can open their mouths wide enough to eat animals that seem much too large for them.
8. Max was surprised to learn that some snakes have sensors between their eyes and nostrils that allow them to "see" the heat of another animal.

page 67

1. apple
2. marble
3. purple
4. beagle
5. freckle
6. simple
7. maple
8. castle

f	p	u	r	p	l	e	h	k	b	i
a	v	e	f	r	e	c	k	l	e	v
s	a	m	a	r	b	l	e	j	r	a
t	p	f	d	a	j	u	y	p	w	g
l	i	z	d	s	i	m	p	l	e	o
e	e	u	d	m	a	a	e	w	k	l

page 68

1. supply
2. python
3. scary
4. easy
5. shy
6. yogurt
7. myth

page 69

1. long **e**
2. short **i**
3. long **i**

4. long **e**
5. **y**

long **e**: quickly, many, especially, country
long **i**: styles, reply
short **i**: pygmies, rhythms
y: yodeling, yodeler, you

page 70

1. circle
2. turtle
3. shark
4. corn
5. letter
6. scarf
7. horse
8. first

page 71

1. c
2. d
3. e
4. b
5. a

Daniel Sullivan was the first person to be known as a horse whisperer. During the 1800s, he became famous in England for helping horses that no one else could help. Some horses were violent. Others had been abused. Daniel was able to calm the horses. They seemed to know they could trust him. Daniel taught two other men the art of horse whispering. Both men wrote books, and more and more people learned about helping troubled horses.

Can you guess how horse whispering got its name? The trainers stand face to face with their horses. People who observed this thought the trainer must be whispering something special to the horse. Actually, horse whisperers just know a lot about horses. They understand these animals better than anyone. It is hard work, and it takes a lot of patience. But most horse whisperers wouldn't dream of doing anything else.

page 72

pear; share
hair; swear
tear; gear
deer; rear
stairs; pairs
bear; stare
spear; smear
silverware; hare
chair; prepare

page 73

hair; wear; aware; cares; prepare; years; nearly; volunteer; hear; share

1. spare
2. engineer
3. dear
4. despair
5. reindeer

page 74

1. applause
2. fable
3. lemon
4. nickel
5. canoe

1. long **i**; long **i**
2. long **e**; **y**
3. long **i**; short **i**; long **e**
4. long **e**; short **i**
5. **y**; long **i**

page 75

1. c
2. b
3. a
4. c
5. b
6. a

1. artist; outdoors; colors
2. painter; careers
3. urged; her; prepare; for; artist
4. Norman; covers; during

page 76

1. discover; miss
2. worry; exclaim
3. bury; suggest; search
4. nod; quit

5. trot; carry; crease

page 77

carry		carried		carrying
	clap	clapped		clapping
	change		changed	changing
	spy	spied		spying
laugh			laughed	laughing
	apply		applied	applying
bike			biked	biking
	shrug		shrugged	shrugging

1. whispered; Answers will vary.
2. studying; Answers will vary.
3. explored; Answers will vary.
4. spied; Answers will vary.

page 78
1. touch
2. reply
3. smile
4. coax
5. buzz
6. cry
7. pass
8. replace

1. cooks
2. scrambles; fries
3. watches
4. mixes
5. carries; shouts; opens

page 79
1. plants; watches
2. worries
3. picks
4. harvests
5. rakes
6. pushes

1. hikes
2. climbs

3. finishes
4. buries

page 80

smart		smarter		smartest
	sad	sadder		saddest
tiny			tinier	tiniest
	bright		brighter	brightest
wet			wetter	wettest
	funny	funnier		funniest
quick			quicker	quickest
	clean	cleaner		cleanest
gentle			gentler	gentlest
	pretty		prettier	prettiest

page 81
1. hottest
2. faster
3. largest
4. longer
5. closest
6. brightest
7. biggest
8. windier

hard **g**: longer; biggest
soft **g**: largest

page 82
1. hurried; Answers will vary.
2. dripped; Answers will vary.
3. carrying; Answers will vary.

1. swims
2. tosses
3. studied
4. clapped
5. finishes

page 83
1. deadliest
2. largest
3. slowest
4. taller

5. sleepiest
6. strangest
7. bigger

page 84
contents; glasses; dishes; pictures; friends; families; animals; wolves; mountains; cliffs; minutes

page 85

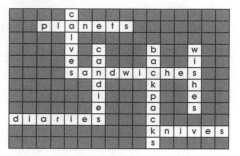

page 86
radios; zoos; photos; videos; rodeos; buffaloes; tomatoes; potatoes; burros

page 87
1. flamingos
2. zeroes
3. igloos
4. pianos
5. shampoos
6. mangoes

1. torpedoes
2. shampoos
3. heroes
4. patios
5. autos
6. mosquitoes
7. solos

One word in the second exercise has the schwa sound. Write the word on the line and circle the vowel that makes the schwa sound.

m(o)squitoes

Answer Key

page 88
1. fish
2. sheep
3. foot
4. mice
5. children

page 89
1. ✓
2. women
3. dice
4. ✓
5. geese
6. deer
7. ✓

1. fish
2. moose
3. child
4. teeth
5. die
6. men
7. trout

page 90
1. the monkey's tail
2. the lion's mane
3. the peacock's feathers
4. Ms. Wells's whistle
5. the zebra's cage

Possible answer: pale tail; Answers will vary.
Possible answer: pain mane; Answers will vary.
Possible answer: lane cage; Answers will vary.

page 91
farmer's; Moses's; paintings'
artist's; Women's; museum's

1. PL

2. PL
3. PL
4. PO

page 92
1. Little Valley Girls' Soccer Team Wins Championship
2. Experts Say Moose's Food Source Quickly Disappearing
3. Storms' High Winds Knock Out Power across Midwest
4. Miners' Strike Surprises Kentucky Town

1. the sheep's wool
2. the players' bats
3. the families' tickets
4. the men's uniforms
5. the McKenzies' dog

page 93
1. PP
2. PL
3. SP
4. SP
5. PL
6. PP

1. a
2. b
3. b
4. a

bu(sh)el   pea(ch)es   (ch)ildren's

page 94

piano	pianos	piano's	pianos'
library	libraries	library's	libraries'
thief	thieves	thief's	thieves'
bicycle	bicycles	bicycle's	bicycles'
goose	geese	goose's	geese's
lady	ladies	lady's	ladies'
roof	roofs	roof's	roofs'
kangaroo	kangaroos	kangaroo's	kangaroos'
boss	bosses	boss's	bosses'
hero	heroes	hero's	heroes'

Rewrite each sentence below, replacing the words in bold with a possessive. Then, underline the plural word or words in the sentence.

1. The **piano teacher of Amira** has given lessons for 40 years.
   Amira's piano teacher has given lessons for 40 years.
2. The **voices of the singers** echoed down the narrow hallways.
   The singers' voices echoed down the narrow hallways.
3. The **keys of the pianos** were yellowed with age.
   The pianos' keys were yellowed with age.
4. The **orchestra of this city** is well known in many countries.
   This city's orchestra is well known in many countries.

page 95
1. states
2. Thousands; islands
3. forests; forests'; companies
4. Potatoes
5. Deer; mice; foxes
6. moose; ponds
7. Autos; moose's; enemies

1. Eskimos
2. daisies
3. geese
4. elves
5. loaves
6. volcanoes
7. brushes
8. ponies

page 96
1. birdcage
2. applesauce
3. fingerprint
4. dollhouse
5. pancake

Possible answers:
backstage; backyard;

Answer Key

backpack; snowfall; snowflake; snowman; snowstorm; firefly; fireman; fireplace; firewood; bathrobe; bathtub; bathroom; seafood; seaweed; seashell

page 97
something; homesick cupcakes; birthday; flowerpots; homemade; afternoon; underwater birdfeeders; pinecones; horseback; thunderstorm; inside; popcorn; fireplace

1. some thing
2. home sick
3. cup cakes
4. birth day
5. flower pots
6. home made
7. after noon
8. under water
9. bird feeders
10. pine cones
11. horse back
12. thunder storm
13. in side
14. pop corn
15. fire place

page 98
1. I
2. they are
3. you'll
4. that is
5. will
6. it will

1. did not; didn't
2. could not; couldn't

3. I am; I'm
4. It is; It's
5. Has not; Hasn't

page 99
It's; aren't; You'll; shouldn't; can't; He's; They're; don't; you'd

1. It is
2. are not
3. You will
4. should not
5. can not
6. He is
7. They are
8. do not
9. you would

page 100
starfish; star and fish fireworks; fire and works wheelchair; wheel and chair horseshoe; horse and shoe sailboat; sail and boat basketball; basket and ball

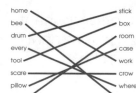

1. homework	home	stick
2. beehive	bee	box
3. drumstick	drum	room
4. everywhere	every	case
5. toolbox	tool	work
6. scarecrow	scare	crow
7. pillowcase	pillow	where
8. classroom	class	hive

page 101
1. could not; o
2. she will; wi
3. I am; a
4. does not; o
5. they are; a

James whistled, and his Border collie, Sadie, raced through the barnyard at top speed. She wasn't as fast as she'd been as a pup, but she had grown calmer and more loyal with every passing year. Together, James and Sadie walked toward the farmhouse.

James could smell the blueberry pie his mother was baking. He pictured her in the kitchen, standing before her stained, worn cookbook. In his mind, he could see a bottle of buttermilk sitting on the counter and some cornbread cooling on the stovetop. Everywhere James looked, he was reminded of something he'd miss. He couldn't believe that there would be no more afternoons chasing Sadie through the cornfields or that he wouldn't go to sleep every night listening to the croak of bullfrogs in the pond.

The time had come for James to go away to school. You'll appreciate it one day," his father had told him. He didn't doubt that his father was right. But that still didn't make it any easier to leave.

page 102
1. uncommon
2. unhurt
3. impossible
4. unsafe
5. impatient
6. disagree
7. invisible
8. disconnect

1. My dog rarely __disobeys__ when he is given a command.
2. Tony is adventurous and is always __unafraid__ of trying new things.
3. If your answer is __incorrect__, the computer will make a beeping sound.
4. We received an __unexpected__ phone call late last night.
5. I don't mean to be __impolite__, but I don't have time to talk right now.

page 103
prewashed
1. Preheat; Precut
2. remix
3. rearrange
4. Preplan; misjudged; reheat
5. reuse; recycle

page 104
1. antislavery; against slavery
2. nonfiction; not fiction
3. antifreeze; against freezing
4. nonstop; without stopping
5. antitheft; against theft
6. nonverbal; not verbal

Answer Key

1. Possible answers: was, his, Annabelle's, hours
2. Possible answers: antislavery, beliefs, ask, squirted, soon, against, sister, sign.

page 105
1. subway
2. supersoft
3. subhuman
4. submarine
5. superstar
6. subzero

1. superpowers
2. superhighways
3. submerged
4. superfine
5. supersized

page 106
hopeless; beautiful; powerful; worthless; pointless; fitful; sleepless; hopeful; cheerful; successful

page 107
1. frozen; Answers will vary.
2. valuable; Answers will vary.
3. breakable; Answers will vary.
4. bitten; Answers will vary.

1. bendable
2. loosen
3. enjoyable
4. brighten

page 108
1. baldness; the state of being bald
2. happiness; the state of being happy
3. citizenship; the state of being a citizen
4. kindness; the state of being kind
5. friendship; the state of being friends
6. ownership; the state of being an owner
7. smoothness; the state of being smooth

page 109
1. sixish
2. advertisement
3. Spanish
4. agreement
5. reddish
6. entertainment

1. arrangement
2. government
3. girlish
4. fiftyish
5. amazement

page 110
1. unlucky
2. subzero
3. impure
4. antipollution
5. indirect
6. nonfiction

unanswered; unexpected; reread; misread; supermarket; preordered; prepaid; subway; nonstop

page 111
1. happiness; Answers will vary.
2. hidden; Answers will vary.
3. agreement; Answers will vary.

endless; brightens; answerable; doubtful; enjoyable

page 112
cricket; 2   banana; 3
alligator; 4   hammer; 2
bike; 1   watermelon; 4

alligator; hammer; watermelon

page 113
1. foot/ball; subject
2. dis/like; cheerful
3. thun/der; subway
4. mis/lead; reuse
5. door/knob; cactus
6. non/stop; kindness

1. Bel/la; sub/way; Fri/day
2. mis/read; re/check; be/fore
3. Dan/ny; bas/ket; home/made; pret/zels
4. dark/ness; with/out; flash/light

page 114

1. second	short		5. comet	short	
2. pilot	long		6. photo	long	
3. major	long		7. metal	short	
4. sliver	short		8. over	long	

Answer Key

1. rhi/no
2. fe/male
3. lem/on
4. ped/al
5. mi/nus

page 115
pen/guins; dol/phins; com/mon; swim/mers; sci/en/tists; flip/pers; fi/gure; un/der/wa/ter; with/out; ef/fort; ve/hi/cles; pro/pel/lers; spa/ces; sa/fer; use/ful; a/round; di/rec/tions; fu/ture; al/low; an/i/mals; Un/like; flex/i/ble; try/ing; ex/per/i/ments; re/build; re/call; an/y/thing; im/i/tates; some/thing

1. scientists
2. boat

page 116
1. zebra; spaceship
2. butterfly; banana
3. toothpaste; secret
4. hat; scream

1. 3; 3
2. 2; 2
3. 3; 3
4. 1; 1
5. 2; 2
6. 4; 4
7. 2; 2
8. 2; 2
9. 4; 4
10. 1; 1

page 117
1 syllable	2 syllables
grin	mis/treat
north	play/pen
press	chim/ney
flame	pu/pil

3 syllables
va/ca/tion
pop/u/lar
mar/vel/ous
ad/ven/ture

1. fa/mous; mil/lions; dol/lars
2. dis/hon/est; cop/y; o/rig/i/nals
3. Re/search/ers
4. dig/i/tal; paint/ing
5. com/put/er; tech/nique
6. com/pare; pic/tures
7. like/ly
8. oth/er; al/so
9. be/fore; ar/tists

page 118
1. odor — smell
2. start — begin
3. brave — courageous
4. present — gift
5. repair — mend

enjoy, children, huge, tugged, yelling, entire, worried, seem, several

page 119
1. give
2. exchange
3. glad
4. tart
5. messy
6. destroy

1. a
2. b
3. c
4. b

5. a
6. c
7. b

1. strange, strong, throw
2. catch, common

page 120
1. North; South
2. hot; cold
3. live; die
4. top; bottom
5. black; white
6. yesterday; today
7. up; down
8. heavier; lighter

page 121
1. eastern
2. few
3. future
4. men
5. after
6. led

1. many
2. past

page 122
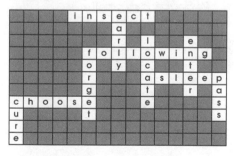

page 123
ordinary; last; observe; smallest; Earth; journey; incredible; started; perfect; evenings; something

Answer Key

page 124
1. gives
2. fix
3. Grab
4. made
5. an example
6. listen
7. right
8. worth
9. piece

page 125
1. sharp; Possible answer: Kerry's costume was a red cape and a pointed hat.
2. pushed; Possible answer: I shoved the stack of books out of the way.
3. coin; Possible answer: We raised a lot of money at the bake sale.
4. late; Possible answer: This movie is three days overdue.
5. stop; Possible answer: Don't quit now, you're almost done!
6. injury; Possible answer: The vet carefully addressed the cat's wound and promised she would be just fine.

pointed, coin

page 126
1. 2, 1, 3
2. 3, 2, 1
3. 3, 2, 1
4. 1, 2, 3
5. 3, 1, 2
6. 2, 3, 1

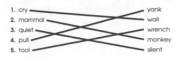

1. cry — monkey
2. mammal — silent
3. quiet — yank
4. pull — wrench
5. tool — wall

page 127
1. carrot
2. Dalmatian
3. juice
4. Atlantic
5. soccer
6. jazz
7. tent
8. shin

page 128
1. untamed; wild
2. Saw; cut
3. fill; pack
4. feeble; weak
5. purpose; meaning
6. own; have
7. consume; eat

1. untied
2. feel
3. record
4. change
5. peak

page 129
1. color, blue, indigo
2. sweets, candy, licorice
3. cloth, towel, dishrag
4. place, country, France

1. hawk
2. diamond
3. watch; clock
4. drums

page 130
horse   cent   deer
ball   pear   cereal

ring   plane   tail

bawl; ball

page 131
aunt; their; made; week; sail; Sea; few; cruise; heard; might; some; too; missed; high; rain; clothes; hear; creak; would; leak; eight; hours; sun; knew; be

page 132
1. b
2. b
3. a
4. a
5. b
6. a
7. b

page 133
Answers will vary. Possible answers:
1. Jimmy dove off the high dive onto the cool waters of the neighbor's pool.
2. Put down your bag and come inside.
3. There are 18 pupils in Ms. Hershey's class.
4. Ebony leaves for school at 7:35 every morning.
5. I like Mr. Dabney because he is kind and has a great sense of humor.
6. When do you think the eggs will hatch?
7. José and Cristina got their dog at the pound.

Which two words in bold contain a diphthong? Circle the diphthong in each word. __down__   __pound__

Answer Key

page 134
1. Ding-dong, bonked
2. Hmmm
3. clomped
4. cheeped; twittered
5. rustled; murmured
6. clanging; buzzing
7. whooshing

1. Did Hannah say as Hannah did?
2. deed
3. toot
4. No lemons, no melon.
5. Ma handed Edna ham.

page 135
1. wipe
2. guestimate
3. scrawl
4. chuckle
5. shimmer
6. clap
7. humongous

1. brunch
2. Internet
3. moped
4. smog

page 136
there; been; weather; seems; our; by; not; great; find; know; whole; for

1. What is today's date?
2. The waiter gave Mom the bill.
3. Mix the batter in the bowl.
4. Your present is in the box.

page 137
1. bird
2. horse
3. human
4. cereal
5. rain
6. thunderstorm

Nurses run; level; Top spot.; racecar; Don't nod.; gag; noon; toot; Rise to vote, sir.; radar

1. d
2. a
3. c
4. b

page 138
1. cherries were as sweet as honey
2. the backyard was dry as a bone
3. snow crunched like popcorn
4. clouds were like puffs of cotton candy
5. the toddler waddled like a penguin

1. the thumping of Rachel's heart; a steady drumbeat
2. tornado; monster
3. baby's teeth; tiny white pearls
4. grass; a velvety carpet
5. sirens; wild shrieks

page 139
1. S
2. M
3. M
4. S
5. M
6. S

Our first night at Greystone Park was incredible. For dinner we cooked juicy burgers over the campfire. The fresh corn on the cob was as yellow as sunshine, and the cherry tomatoes burst in our mouths like tiny water balloons. After dinner, we sat quietly in the darkness. Wisps of smoke from the fire danced into the sky like twirling and leaping ballerinas. At home, I'd probably be watching TV or playing on the computer, but I don't miss either of those things here. The darkness is a thick warm blanket that makes me feel cozy and safe with my family.

It's so much louder here than it is outside our apartment. Somehow, though, the night sounds of the woods are a soothing lullaby. Sleep washes over me like a wave, and I finally stop fighting to stay awake.

page 140
1. k
2. i
3. c
4. j
5. b
6. h
7. e
8. d
9. g
10. f
11. a

day, hay, stay

page 141
we'd all be in the same boat; stick together; dawned on; worth sticking out her neck for; something up his sleeve; a slim chance; drives a hard bargain

page 142
1. The warm chicken noodle soup was as comforting as a hug.
2. The tree branches were like fingers that reached toward the old house.
3. The terrible secret was a heavy load that Cassie carried with her.
4. The morning sun was a cheery invitation for Jack to get up.
5. The flock of blackbirds burst into the sky like a handful of confetti.

1. Answers will vary.
2. Answers will vary.
3. Answers will vary.

Answer Key

4. Answers will vary.

1. On the lines, write three words that begin or end with a digraph.
   Possible answers:
   chicken, comforting, cheery, with, flock, blackbirds

2. Which word contains a vowel diphthong? Circle the diphthong.
   h(ou)se

page 143
1. dead to the world
2. neck and neck
3. all in the same boat
4. set someone straight
5. on cloud nine
6. plain as the nose on his/her face
7. felt like a million dollars
8. down in the dumps
9. stole the spotlight

1. Answers will vary.
2. Answers will vary.
3. Answers will vary.
4. Answers will vary.

page 144
1. mist
2. nice
3. pizza
4. squat
5. fabulous
6. dispatch
7. flounder

1. 3, 2, 1
2. 2, 1, 3
3. 1, 3, 2
4. 3, 2, 1
5. 2, 3, 1
6. 2, 3, 1

page 145
1. accordion
2. African
3. anyone
4. band
5. became
6. blues
7. bouncy
8. Cajun
9. Creole
10. fingers
11. first
12. folk
13. form
14. jazz
15. popular
16. snapping
17. tapping
18. toes
19. washboard
20. zydeco

accordion, fingers, first, form, popular, washboard

page 146
1. b
2. c
3. b
4. c
5. a
6. b

1. Answers will vary.
2. Answers will vary.
3. Answers will vary.
4. Answers will vary.
5. Answers will vary.

page 147
1. page 97
2. page 98
3. page 220
4. page 97
5. page 97
6. page 222
7. page 220
8. page 98
9. page 222
10. page 97
11. page 220
12. page 98
13. page 222
14. page 98

trade—transform
traffic
tragedy
trampoline

sandpaper—Saturday
sandwich
sank
sari

page 148
1. sunny
2. laugh
3. sandwich
4. whisper
5. busy
6. buzz
7. split
8. mango

1. 2
2. the first
3. noun

page 149
sport, judge, success, weigh, compare, draw, rule, tell, professional, win, young

page 150
Atlantis: The Last Empire
Because of Winn-Dixie
The Incredibles
The Princess Bride
Robots

The Rookie
The Secret of Roan Inish
Spy Kids
The Wizard of Oz

1. dreamy, drench, dress, driftwood
2. honest, honey, hood, hook
3. spicy, spider, spindle, spoil
4. breed, brew, bridle, broccoli
5. model, moist, mold, mole

page 151
monument—more
moon
moor
moral

moss—mound
motor
motel
motto

mourn—muffin
mud
mouse
mown

1. match, maybe, meadow
2. matches
3. maybe
4. the first

1. city
2. clap
3. peacock
4. bunch
5. mosquito
6. yell

page 152
1. f
2. d
3. j
4. a
5. h
6. c
7. b
8. e
9. i
10. g

page 153
1. circus
2. elephant
3. juggler
4. tightrope
5. lion
6. clown
7. acrobat

1. sailboat; male
2. gentle; justice
3. Clare; wear
4. oyster; voyage
5. amuse; cute

Possible answers: /s/ sailboat, justice, oyster, toast, custom
/z/ amuse

page 154
slave, often, Once, been, world, against, everywhere, Large, friend, became, when, about, afraid, thought, stood, right

page 155
1. gentle
2. totem
3. weigh
4. enough
5. future

1. Imagine
2. like; creature; Asia
3. lived; million
4. Ice; disease
5. Some; claim; remote

page 156
1. /sōl jer/
2. /hŏk ē/
3. /rū bē/
4. /e round/
5. /ri fyūz/
6. /pe līs/
7. / me skē tō/
8. /roi el/
9. /skwē kē/
10. /pe tō tō/

1. a
2. a
3. b
4. a
5. b
6. b
7. a
8. b

page 157
Emmanuel strolled **along** (e lōng) the sidewalk in front of his school, watching for his friend Matt. **Several** (sev′er el) days each week, they met after school and walked **together** (te geth′er) to the rec center to play chess. Emmanuel preferred having **plenty** (plen′tē) of time to think about each move, but Matt liked it **better** (bet′er) when they used the clock.

Suddenly, Matt came **running** (run′ing) out of the school's front door. Matt **explained** (ik splānd) that he had just **spoken** (spō′ken) to Mr. Sanchez, the **principal** (prin′se pel). He had agreed to join Emmanuel and Matt on **Thursdays** (thūrz′dāz) to teach them new chess strategies. With a little help, the boys felt sure their game would improve in no time.

Some multiple-meaning words are spelled the same but pronounced differently. The word record can be pronounced /rek′erd/ or /ri kōrd/. The meaning is different depending on the accents and pronunciation.

Underline the respelling that correctly completes each sentence below.
1. What time will Mr. Klein (/pri zent′/, /prez′ent/) his speech?
2. Kyle was stationed in the (/di zūrt′/, /dez′ert/) for two years.
3. Who will (/ken dukt′/, /kŏn′dukt/) the orchestra this year?
4. "I (/ob′jikt/, /eb jekt′/)," said the judge, pounding his gavel.
5. Santhe's favorite (/sub′jikt/, /seb jekt′/) is English, but she likes science, too.

page 158
1. /ā/
2. this, smooth
3. /i/
4. su, ge
5. ō
6. a, e, i, o, u

Answer Key

1. every
2. enjoy
3. said; native
4. grown; bogs; country
5. fields
6. float

page 159

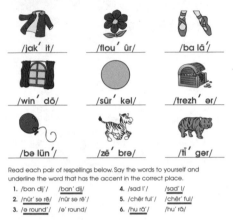

/jak′ it/   /flou′ ûr/   /ba lā′/

/win′ dō/   /sûr′ kəl/   /trezh′ ər/

/bə lün′/   /zē′ brə/   /tī′ gər/

Read each pair of respellings below. Say the words to yourself and
underline the word that has the accent in the correct place.

1. /ban dij′/   /ban′ dij/
2. /nûr′ sə rē/   /nûr sə rē′/
3. /ə round′/   /ə′ round/
4. /sad l′/   /sad′ l/
5. /cher ful′/   /chêr′ ful/
6. /hu rā′/   /hu′ rā/